The Time of My Life
My Coast 2 Coast Adventure

By
Clarence Bechter

Copyright © 2021 by Clarence Bechter

All rights reserved. No part of this book may be reproduced or transmitted in any form or by any means without written permission from the author.

ISBN: 978-1-964712-15-4

3rd printing

Printed in USA Books

Acknowledgements

I would like to thank my wife Mary for hours upon hours of help with typing my journal and the ultimate creation of this book.

I would also like to thank Leslie Haynam for her endless hours of editing, proofreading and layout help.

How many times in life have you heard some variation of this comment?
"I wish I would have…." Please don't just dream.
If you think about it more often than you can count, it's something that will keep tugging at you. Grab it and try. You will never know, until you try.

Table of Contents

Acknowledgements ii

Introduction vii

Journal Day 1 1

Journal Day 2 4

Journal Day 3 6

Journal Day 4 9

Journal Day 5 12

Journal Day 6 15

Journal Day 7 17

Journal Day 8 19

Journal Day 9 22

Journal Day 10 25

Journal Day 11 28

Journal Day 12 30

Journal Day 13 33

Journal Day 14 36

Journal Day 15 38

Journal Day 16 40

Journal Day 17 43

Journal Day 18 46

Journal Day 19 49

Journal Day 20 52

Journal Day 21 54

Journal Day 22 57

Journal Day 23 60

Journal Day 24 63
Journal Day 25 66
Journal Day 26 69
Journal Day 27 72
Journal Day 28 75
Journal Day 29 77
Journal Day 30 80
Journal Day 31 82
Journal Day 32 85
Journal Day 33 88
Journal Day 34 90
Journal Day 35 92
Journal Day 36 95
Journal Day 37 98
Journal Day 38 102
Journal Day 39 105
Journal Day 40 107
Journal Day 41 110
Journal Day 42 112
Journal Day 43 115
Journal Day 44 120
Journal Day 45 125
Journal Day 46 128
Journal Day 47 130
Journal Day 48 133
Journal Day 49 135
Journal Day 50 137

Journal Day 51 139

Journal Day 52 145

POST RIDE REFLECTION April 23 - May 1, 2019 151

Introduction

Bubba's Pampered Pedalers

March 2, 2019 to April 22, 2019

From the Pacific Ocean to the Atlantic Ocean

A little over a year before doing this ride, my wife Mary gave me her blessing to live out my dream of pedaling my bicycle across the United States. One can't live out a dream by saying what if this happens or what if that happens… you just have to do it. You have to believe in yourself and have faith. Once Mary agreed, the planning started and what a life-changing experience it turned out to be.

This book is a journal of my experiences and perceptions as I pedaled my bicycle across the United States. The 2019 C2C tour was truly an adventure that turned strangers into a family of riders. This is the kind of gift you give yourself for the future… for the memories you make and the friends you would never have known without the experience.

Here are some interesting facts concerning the 2019 C2C tour:

44 riders started

42 finished

11 female

33 male

65 average age

44 youngest rider

73 oldest rider

17 states represented

7 riders from Ohio (the most represented state on this tour)

3 countries represented - the United States, Canada & Germany

3,000 total miles

8 states toured: California, Arizona, New Mexico, Texas, Louisiana, Mississippi, Alabama and Florida.

71,207 feet elevation gain (13.5 vertical miles)

1,582 feet daily average gain

65 daily average miles

45 pedaling days

7 rest days

2,160,982 tire rotations

Yes, over two million rotations.

My plan started with a lot of mental and physical training. I read a book that stated a trip like this is 70% mental and 30% physical, so this 68-year-old had some organizing to do to get to my goal. First on my list was to purchase a bike.

Most long-distance riders choose a typical road bike. So, guess what I had never ridden? Yes, a road bike. They looked uncomfortable with the riders all bent way over the handlebars. Later I changed my tune on this theory. Our nephew Tim owns a Cannondale and we are about the same size, so he challenged me to try his bike. This was a new style of riding for me. But, the low-profile rider position proved to be more aerodynamic and the clipped-in pedals helped with the power of the upstroke. One thing I became aware of almost instantly was that you can develop more power with a road bike. With this being decided, I visited bike shops in the Akron, Ohio area. I needed hand-on experience and I road-tested a Trek, a Cannondale and a Jamis.

I decided on a Jamis Renegade. This was custom fitted for me at Falls Wheel and Wrench in Cuyahoga Falls, Ohio by the owner, Bob. Once I had my bike, I ventured out on many trails, roads and hills.

These rides were about learning to ride the bike well, but they also helped to condition my bottom.

A few of my riding friends encouraged me and gave me the confidence that I was a strong rider. The other members of the Akron 60 Strong group also boosted my confidence level. Joining the Green, Ohio YMCA and taking cycling lessons from Marie on Saturday mornings, and going back on my own two to three days a week and swimming helped to condition my body for the ride.

Eight months prior to my coast to coast ride, in August of 2018, I summited Mount Whitney in California. The 22 mile hike takes you up 14,508 feet to the highest peak in the lower 48 states. The very next month I pedaled from Washington,

D.C. to Pittsburgh, PA (335 miles) on my Giant hybrid. At that point, I felt ready. I had done everything I could do to prepare myself to complete the ride from coast to coast.

Day-by-Day Itinerary for Bubba's Pampered Pedalers 2019 Coast-to-Coast Bicycling Tour

Day		Date	Start	End	Miles	Type	Lodging Name
	Fri	1-Mar	San Diego, CA	San Diego, CA		Hotel	Ocean Villa Inn
1	Sat	2-Mar	San Diego, CA	Alpine, CA	37	Hotel	unknown: "shuttle to camp"
2	Sun	3-Mar	Alpine, CA	Jacumba, CA	45	Hotel	Jacumba Hot Springs Resort
3	Mon	4-Mar	Jacumba, CA	Calexico, CA	51	Indoor	Calexico Mission School
4	Tue	5-Mar	Calexico, CA	Yuma, AZ	65	Indoor	Natl Guard Armory
5	Wed	6-Mar	Yuma, AZ	Dateland, AZ	70	Camp	Dateland RV Park
6	Thu	7-Mar	Dateland, AZ	Gila Bend, AZ	52	Camp	Gila Bend KOA
7	Fri	8-Mar	Gila Bend, AZ	Casa Grande, AZ	87	Camp	High Chaparral RV Park
8	Sat	9-Mar	Casa Grande, AZ	Catalina, AZ	55	Camp	Catalina State Park
9	Sun	10-Mar	Catalina, AZ	Catalina, AZ		Camp	Catalina State Park
10	Mon	11-Mar	Catalina, AZ	Tucson, AZ	44	Camp	Adventure Bound RV Resort
11	Tue	12-Mar	Tucson, AZ	Tombstone, AZ	73	Hotel	Landmark Lookout Lodge
12	Wed	13-Mar	Tombstone, AZ	Douglas, AZ	50	Hotel	Gadsden Hotel
13	Thu	14-Mar	Douglas, AZ	Rodeo, NM	55	Indoor	Chiricahua Mountain Lodge
14	Fri	15-Mar	Rodeo, NM	Columbus, NM	92	Indoor	Columbus Elementary School
15	Sat	16-Mar	Columbus, NM	Columbus, NM		Indoor	Columbus Elementary School
16	Sun	17-Mar	Columbus, NM	El Paso, TX	75	Hotel	Quality Suites
17	Mon	18-Mar	El Paso, TX	Ft. Hancock, TX	61	Indoor	Ft. Hancock High School
18	Tue	19-Mar	Ft. Hancock, TX	Van Horn, TX	74	Camp	Van Horn RV Park
19	Wed	20-Mar	Van Horn, TX	Marfa, TX	73	Indoor	Marfa Activity Center
20	Thu	21-Mar	Marfa, TX	Marathon, TX	57	Camp	Marathon RV Park
21	Fri	22-Mar	Marathon, TX	Marathon, TX		Camp	Marathon RV Park
22	Sat	23-Mar	Marathon, TX	Sanderson, TX	56	Indoor	Sanderson High School
23	Sun	24-Mar	Sanderson, TX	Comstock, TX	82	Camp	Seminole Canyon State Park
24	Mon	25-Mar	Comstock, TX	Brackettville, TX	73	Camp	Ft. Clark Springs Camping World
25	Tue	26-Mar	Brackettville, TX	Concan, TX	74	Cabin/Car	Yeargan's Riverbed Resort
26	Wed	27-Mar	Concan, TX	Concan, TX		Cabin/Car	Yeargan's Riverbed Resort
27	Thu	28-Mar	Concan, TX	Kerrville, TX	73	Camp	Kerrville Schreiner Park
28	Fri	29-Mar	Kerrville, TX	Blanco, TX	59	Camp	Blanco State Park
29	Sat	30-Mar	Blanco, TX	Lockhart, TX	63	Camp	Lockhart State Park
30	Sun	31-Mar	Lockhart, TX	La Grange, TX	60	Indoor	Randolph Recreation Center
31	Mon	1-Apr	La Grange, TX	Richards, TX	89	Camp	Mexican Hill Ranch
32	Tue	2-Apr	Richards, TX	Richards, TX		Camp	Mexican Hill Ranch
33	Wed	3-Apr	Richards, TX	Shepherd, TX	62	Camp	Shepherd Sanctuary
34	Thu	4-Apr	Shepherd, TX	Silsbee, TX	61	Camp	Red Cloud RV Park
35	Fri	5-Apr	Silsbee, TX	DeRidder, LA	73	Hotel	Quality Inn
36	Sat	6-Apr	DeRidder, LA	Opelousas, LA	91	Hotel	Holiday Inn
37	Sun	7-Apr	Opelousas, LA	St. Francisville, LA	68	Camp	Camp Marydale
38	Mon	8-Apr	St. Francisville, LA	St. Francisville, LA		Camp	Camp Marydale
39	Tue	9-Apr	St. Francisville, LA	Franklinton, LA	86	Indoor/Ca	Hillcrest Baptist Church
40	Wed	10-Apr	Franklinton, LA	Poplarville, MS	45	Indoor	Poplarville Natl Guard Armory
41	Thu	11-Apr	Poplarville, MS	Ocean Springs, MS	70	Hotel	Super8 Motel
42	Fri	12-Apr	Ocean Springs, MS	Dauphin Island, AL	78	Camp	Dauphin Island Park Campground
43	Sat	13-Apr	Dauphin Island, AL	Dauphin Island, AL		Camp	Dauphin Island Park Campground
44	Sun	14-Apr	Dauphin Island, AL	Pensacola, FL	55	Indoor	Bear Levin Studer YMCA
45	Mon	15-Apr	Pensacola, FL	Milton, FL	31	Camp	KOA
46	Tue	16-Apr	Milton, FL	DeFuniak Springs, FL	54	Camp	SunsetKing RV Resort
47	Wed	17-Apr	DeFuniak Springs, FL	Marianna, FL	69	Camp	Arrowhead Camp Resort
48	Thu	18-Apr	Marianna, FL	Tallahassee, FL	85	Hotel	Quality Inn
49	Fri	19-Apr	Tallahassee, FL	Live Oak, FL	77	Indoor	Suwannee County Fairgrounds
50	Sat	20-Apr	Live Oak, FL	Gainesville, FL	81	Indoor	North Central Florida YMCA
51	Sun	21-Apr	Gainesville, FL	Palatka, FL	53	Indoor	Natl Guard Armory
52	Mon	22-Apr	Palatka, FL	St. Augustine, FL	36	Hotel	Marriott Courtyard, Beach

Total Miles: 2920   Avg Miles/Day: 65   Days: 45

March 2, 2019 – San Diego, California

THE TIME OF MY LIFE

JOURNAL DAY 1

Saturday, March 2, 2019

San Diego, California to Alpine California

37 miles

Looking eastward from the beach in San Diego, my heart is racing with excitement for this 3,000 mile bicycle trip of a lifetime. Today is our first riding day. All 44 riders converge in the breakfast room, boy what a crowd. Remember the song, "It Never Rains in Sunny Southern California?" Well today it's pouring rain.

Bubba has our wheel dipping in the Pacific at 9:00 am, at Dog Beach, a couple hundred yards from our Ocean Villa Hotel. After several group pictures, Bubba states he has two emotional days, "today and the last day." The lump Bubba has in his throat is the same for the whole group. None of us really know what is ahead of us as we cross this vast country.

Our ride starts on a 3.7 mile bike trail along the San Diego River. We pass Qualcomm Stadium where the San Diego Chargers used to play. Now the road riding starts with many left and right turns. We climb up the foothills of the mountains ahead of us. Once we are into the mountains, there are many curves and valleys all day long. We enter the Friar Junipero Serra County Park in Alpine, and our first SAG stop is just ahead. SAG stands for support, assistance, and gear. At a SAG stop our support team has set up a canopy with chairs and tables with fruit and many snack items. They make wraps for us and offer Gatorade concentrate to mix with our water. At the stop I have a peanut butter and jelly wrap, a banana and a pickle, with a shot of pickle juice in a Dixie cup. All this will help with the leg cramping, which is a concern for some of us. As we filter out of the SAG stop, we continue pedaling up the mountains as the rains come down. An hour and a half later our lunch stop is at Roberto's Taco Shop. I order a burrito and when it arrives on my plate it is 6 x 16 inches long. I have lunch with Terri and Bob from Colorado. They are the only tandem bike riders.

After lunch we are now riding on historic Route 80. Today's total climb in elevation is 2925 feet. After entering an area of steep switchbacks my right leg starts to cramp up. I immediately get off my bike and start walking off the cramp while proceeding forward. Our destination today is McDonalds in Alpine. Upon arriving our bikes are loaded into trailers and anchored. We are all shuttled to our next two night stay in Jacumba Springs, some 45 miles away to the east. Our clothes are still damp from the morning rain and the air is cool. The reason for the shuttle is, in previous years the tour had camped in this area and always experienced very cold nights because of the altitude. Now the tour has a hotel room for the first two nights; thank goodness because these 2 days prove to be our toughest days through the mountains.

Friar Junipero Serra County Park

Our chef Anne is traveling with us all the way. She and her husband Serge are from Culinary Insider. Anne has already made hot mushroom soup that is ready to serve when we arrive. Our rooms are ready for us, all we have to do is see Bubba's assistant, Snowflake, for our key. Biker Bill from North Carolina is my roommate for these next two nights. After a nice hot shower, we all file outside for our dinner meal where Anne will always have two entrees and a vegan option for some who would choose. We all go back inside to eat because the sun is going down along with the temperature. The US / Mexico border is a short walking distance away.

Each night after dinner and during dessert, Bubba has a short riders meeting that includes passing out route sheets and explaining in detail anything such as SAG stops, railroad crossings, best lunch stops, and points of interest. The SAG team is responsible for putting biodegradable bright pink fluorescent arrows on the roads for routing. Bubba mentions that the first two days are the toughest because of the elevation climbs and also tells us if we make it through these first 2 days, we will probably make it the rest of the way.

After the meeting, most of us walk back to our rooms to get ready for day two. Regarding day two, we had a sneak preview because we had been shuttled on some of the same roads as tomorrow's route.

Never in my wildest dreams did I think at my age this kind of trip could be a reality.

CLARENCE BECHTER

Journal Day 2

Sunday, March 3, 2019

Alpine, California to Jacumba Springs, California

45 miles

Waking up to cool desert temperatures, we all file outside to the serving line for breakfast. Anne has a spread of hot oatmeal with nuts, berries, sugar, coconut, and brown sugar. There is also a mix of fruits - apples, oranges, and bananas, and a large assortment of breads, bagels, and pastries. We also find butter, cream cheese, and peanut butter. For drinks we have cranberry and orange juices, coffee and hot water for cocoa or tea. I read in a book that for every hour pedaled, a biker burns approximately 540 calories.

After breakfast we are shuttled to the McDonalds in Alpine, 45 miles away where our bikes are waiting for us. Our riding day starts in a cold rain while reaching 4,000 ft in altitude. Fun fact: for every 1000 feet in elevation gain, the temperature decreases 5 degrees. Our ride today will take us through a border checkpoint. This is the same checkpoint Mary and I went through in August of 2018. If you like to pedal up mountains, this day will be your lucky day. I always try to think of other things because of the 4,521 feet of elevation climb. We have two SAG check ins, the first at mile 17.4 and the second at mile 34, at Live Oak Market where we eat lunch. We are crossing over the Pacific Crest Trail (PCT just after Live Oak Springs Road (reference point). This is a good day for most everyone, I personally try to consume 5 quarts of liquid not counting SAG stops. A few miles before reaching Jacumba Springs we ride alongside the border fence, at times it is 200 yards to our right. The clouds lift and it becomes sunny and pleasant. This is a great way to end our day. Upon arriving at Jacumba Springs, Anne and Serge are setting up snacks for us. At 6:00 pm we have dinn er and then our daily rider meeting.

THE TIME OF MY LIFE

Riding through the Desert

A Typical SAG Stop

Journal Day 3

Monday, March 4, 2019

Jacumba Springs, California to Calexico, California

51 miles

We all have the same rooms we had the night before, so this is nice. Breakfast for me this morning is oatmeal, coconut, brown sugar and a banana, eggs with spinach, a piece of toast with peanut butter and Smucker's strawberry jelly. Upon leaving the Jacumba Springs Resort, eight of us ride five blocks down to town in Jacumba to an open-air railroad museum. We see a few vintage rail cars and one engine. Returning back on the route for the day, the desert is very cool and we have a smooth shoulder to ride on, which makes the ride more enjoyable. After five miles we have a right turn onto Interstate 8. The first three miles are a steady 3% uphill grade. Ahead of us is what Bubba spoke about in the riders meeting last night, a fast downhill grade of seven miles with switchbacks and side winds that sometimes may lean you over 15 to 20 degrees. I pass two riders who choose to walk for safety reasons. At one point I reach 36 miles per hour downhill! This is quite an experience of riding down a mountain, with semi-trucks and cars passing, while dealing with the cross winds all at the same time. Half way down the mountain I see Toph on the side of the road with a flat. No worries, Ken and Greg are there to assist him.

Coming down the mountain on a 7 mile downward descent, there is nothing but desert for as far as I can see. I check the temperature on my phone and it is now 80 degrees. We went from 3,200 feet to below sea level in about an hour's time.

Exiting interstate 8 we have a SAG check in at the Red Feather Cafe, in Ocotillo, California which is a mile away from our route. Riding a few more miles we enter what they refer to as "The Salad Bowl of America." The Imperial Valley has perfect soil for growing romaine lettuce, cabbage, broccoli and celery. Here is where many of the vegetables are grown, picked, packaged and shipped to grocery stores across the United States. The water they use to irrigate comes from the Colorado River. There is an abundance of water this year from the snow melt in the Rocky Mountains.

This is a good weather day for everyone, going up a mountain range and flying down the east side and then into the desert. I personally drink five quarts of liquid, not counting what I drink at the SAG stop.

Riding along CA-98E /Yuma cut off there is a sandy road on our right, this is where the border patrol drags the parallel road with tires. The border patrol returns later to look for foot prints from the illegals trying to cross the border. This area also has hundreds of wind turbines and solar panels to produce a vast amount of electricity.

Now the temperature is approaching the 80s with full sun, what a glorious day to ride. We have flat smooth desert roads to pedal on with little wind. We arrive early and cannot get into the Seventh Day Adventist school until 3:05 pm. A small group of us go to a local coffee shop where we will pass the time. A large majority of the high school students from this school come across the border every day for their education. The students make us dinner. The posted menu is bean soup, rice tamales, salad, ice tea, water and cookies for dessert. If you are wondering, yes, most of us have a second helping.

After dinner, but during dessert Bubba has a riders meeting where he introduces the students who prepared our meal, and asks them what their plans are after graduation. When the students are done we have a speaker who talks about the southern Arizona area we are riding through, next to the Mexico border. The Seventh Day Adventist school is 50 ft from the Mexican border fence. Our next speaker explains how the area became so fertile and briefly touches on the Yuma Territorial prison that dates back to July 1st, 1876.

Coach is our bike mechanic on this trip. He rode coast to coast with Bubba in 2015. I ask him if he has time to look at my disc brakes, they are feeling a little soft because of the long descents in the last couple days. He does. In the mornings Coach waits until everyone leaves and he will ride out to the first SAG stop and usually waits until most leave and then will leap frog on the road looking for riders who may need assistance.

We stay in the school gymnasium tonight. We will have our first DSL, which stands for dirty stinking laundry, which we will place into marked bins. Tomorrow the SAG team will go to the laundromat and wash, dry, fold and return our clean laundry to us after dinner, this service is done approximately every four days. I write down the items turned in on my log sheet and when picking them up, they are checked off the list. Some of the other coasters take pictures of their laundry.

When staying in a group setting, such as a gymnasium, community center or National Guard Armory, Coach makes the announcement at 8:50 pm that the lights will be turned out tonight promptly at 9:00 pm. Good night from Calexico, California.

U.S. Mexico Border

JOURNAL DAY 4

Tuesday, March 5, 2019

Calexico, California to Yuma, Arizona

65 miles

Last night we slept in the Seventh Day Adventist School gym. The students make us breakfast and begin serving at 7 am. Remember, most of these kids had to wake up at 4:30 am to cross the border. These students range in age from 14-16 years old. What a great group of kids they are.

Today, I will ride with Otto from Germany. To prepare for the day, we both lather up with 50 spf suntan lotion and I also put on a pair of arm sleeves. After a couple of hours, the desert heat is rising as we pedal on Interstate 8. The speed limit is 80 mph. Most traffic moves over to the left lane, the single and double semi-trucks create a wind and a vacuum effect when they pass us. We exit the freeway on Ogilby Rd. and then make a right turn on to Center of The World Drive. This is the road I read about before leaving on the trip. This road is just chip and seal and very rough. It is so rough I actually chew two sticks of gum to keep my teeth from chattering together. Our SAG stop for lunch is at Center of The World where a fellow by the name of Jacques-Andre had a monument built, a pyramid and chapel with the history of the world. This would be quite an interesting place to come back to someday.

After lunch, we are back on Interstate 8 for one exit. You may be wondering why we were allowed on the Interstate and the answer is - if no other roads run parallel to the interstate we are allowed to ride on the shoulder. Bubba has a rule that we have to get off at every exit for safety reasons and then get back on, so as not to cross traffic at any time. Today is a great day to ride, no clouds and full sun. I drink five quarts of liquid not counting lunch and SAG stops. While riding in the desert you don't perspire much because of the low humidity.

But it just sucks the moisture out of you. It is best to keep well hydrated; hydration will also help you avoid leg cramps.

Today, one of the riders has an accident and injures his hand. Bubba takes Rick to the hospital where he finds out his hand is indeed broken. This will end his bike ride for this year. He vows to try again in 2020. We were just getting to know Rick and wish him the best. At dinner, a giant card is placed on a table so we can all sign it for him.

While riding to our overnight accommodations, several of us make an incorrect turn and pedal a mile and a half out of our way. At this point we pull out our cell phones to find the directions to our overnight stop at the National Guard Armory in Yuma, Arizona.

Yuma has an extensive history of Native trails along with the Yuma Territorial Prison which was open from 1806-1909. During 1540 the Spanish Explorers also came to this area looking for gold. This entire region has a 12-month growing season, so the farming business never has a down time. To grow in the desert condition the farmers use a vertical siphon to get the water from the Colorado River for their crops.

Upon arriving at the National Guard Armory, Anne and Serge have snacks set out for us at 4:00, and our laundry is already cleaned and folded on 3 tables ready for us to pick up. At 6:00 our dinner consists of chicken, sausage, sauerkraut, snap peas, quinoa, bread and salad. Anne also has Haagen Dazs ice cream for dessert. Always after dinner Bubba has a riders meeting to inform us of our ride for the next day.

Our elevation gain today was 978.

THE TIME OF MY LIFE

Calexico, California

Route 8 in Arizona

Journal Day 5

Wednesday, March 6, 2019

Yuma, Arizona to Dateland, Arizona

70 miles

We have a great stay at the National Guard Armory and wake up to perfect weather on our first full day in Arizona. Shortly after the crack of dawn we are starting out as the sun is directly in our faces. My bike helmet had no bill when I bought it. I am very glad Mary cut the bill off of an extra hat, sewed and used velcro to attach it to the inside of my helmet. This helps immensely on sunny and rainy days.

Today we have 2 full SAG stops, a full SAG is where Bubba provides anything and everything you could need, such as peanut butter wraps with pickles, bananas, Nutella, cookies, candy, fruit, water, Gatorade powder mix and soda. Also, comfortable chairs are set up; this is really being pampered. The forecast for today is a high of 85 degrees.

I am riding with a group of four riders today, and one of them is Otto from Germany. He speaks very good English. Otto lives in the region close to Lake Constance in Lauren, Germany or the Bodensee and that is also where he gets his purified house water. After talking to him at SAG and lunch stops, I mention the town where my family is from, a town called Hittisau, Austria. Otto knew where that was because he had visited there for skiing and mountain hiking.

Upon leaving the National Guard Armory, we are all in a line and make an incorrect turn that takes us 2 miles out of our way. After realizing this, 4 cell phones come out and we finally locate Bubba's route without much delay.

Our lunch stop is at Jac's Whistle Stop Cafe in Tacna, Arizona. It feels good to get out of the desert heat. During this ride we are passing thousands of acres of produce which is known as the Salad Bowl of

America. The farm workers pick, wash, and box all types of produce by hand. It's hard to fathom bending over the entire day picking produce then doing it again the next day. But someone has to do the job and I do appreciate them, and I am very thankful for what they do.

Today is a perfect weather day and all 43 coasters sure are glad we are past the mountain ranges east of San Diego. Just outside of Date land RV Park, our first night camping, Bubba suggests we stop at Date land Truck stop for a date shake. I pay $5 for a small date shake and it is the best tasting shake after a 70 mile ride. The campground is 1/4 mile away and there are about 45 tents set up with numbers on them. Now all the riders have to do is find their tent number, mine is 82. After finding my tent, I lean my bike next to a willow tree and walk over to my tent. I remove my shoes, unzip my tent and step inside, to find my air mattress blown up and three pieces of luggage inside the tent. This is what pampering is all about. You are probably wondering who does the majority of the pampering? The answer is the "WOLF PACK." They are a crew of 3 guys and 2 gals under the age of 26. They work incredibly hard to make our trip across America as comfortable as possible. Many thanks, you are much appreciated Wolf Pack.

The RV Park where we are staying is in the middle of the desert which means it is all sand. The Interstate and the railroad tracks are each less than a mile away from our camping location. We have three hot showers in camp, there are no complaints, even if you have to wait in a short line.

At the start of today, I spotted two mountains due east and guessed them to be about 30 miles away. At lunch time we were close to them and by dinner they were 35 miles west of us which means we rode for 70 miles and we never lost sight of them for the entire day.

At this point in the trip we are beginning to bond. We are all living A DREAM, just being a large group of mostly senior citizens, riding our bicycles across the USA.

Anne's Typical Afternoon Snack

Camping in Dateland, Arizona

THE TIME OF MY LIFE

JOURNAL DAY 6

Thursday, March 7, 2019

Dateland, Arizona to Gila Bend, Arizona

52 miles

Breakfast this morning is spinach and eggs, oatmeal with all the fixings, bagels, toast, peanut butter, jellies, fruit, coffee, juice and assorted pastries. Today we will ride with 668 ft. of elevation gain and 318 feet of decline. This is a day of just pedaling and enjoying the ride and scenery of the mountains.

Shortly after leaving the Dateland RV Park we start our ride on Interstate 8 eastbound. Directly in front of us is the sunrise over the mountains, it is very picturesque. Interstate 8 has a wide shoulder and smooth pavement, you have to watch for steel wire from tire tread remnants. There is also lots of glass, nails, screws, rocks and of all things, coins. Most of the time Zach is looking for roadside license plates that he collects.

Whenever we ride on an Interstate, Bubba always has us get off at every exit and get back on with the flow of traffic, so we never cross traffic from cars getting on the Interstate. 50% of our ride today is on the interstate. We also are riding on a frontage road that is extremely rough and slow going. A frontage road runs parallel to a main road or highway, giving access to houses and businesses.

The Saguaro cactus are absolutely beautiful in the Sonoran Desert. They can grow as high as 40 feet. As I am pedaling by, I picture John Wayne doing the same thing except on his horse. The Sonoran Desert in the American Southwest is about 100,000 square miles.

Our lunch stop is at Sophia's at mile 49.2. Bubba always gives us lunch suggestions, some historical points of interest and photo opportunities. These suggestions are on our rider sheets they pass out to us, the evening before at our riders meetings.

Today we pass thousands of acres of green fields with alfalfa, and many different kinds of vegetables growing. We briefly stop and talk to one of the growers and he assures us even though this is a desert, if he has water he can grow anything. Standing here and scanning the acres of green, there is no recognizable civilization, as far as your eye could see in all directions.

Tonight, we are staying at the Gila Bend Campground. As I ride into the campground I look for my #82 tent. I spot my tent along a fence row with a pea gravel base. Entering the tent, I spot my luggage which is always placed inside. I pull out what I need to make up my bed and get ready for the next day. Once I'm finished, I realize I have time to go to the pool for a swim. This particular KOA Campground has a magnificent community center, with a large screen TV, library books, sofas and several chairs, and also a full size kitchen where we will eat our next two meals.

SAG Stop

After the swim, a few of us walk over to the 'Pampered Zone' where we can choose from Ravioli, Tortellini and corn chips, hummus and celery. This is considered a snack. Snacks are always served at 4:00 every day. On cooler days, Anne will make us HOT soup. Anne always gives us a variety of cheeses, assorted crackers and hummus. This is a welcome treat after a long riding day.

After dinner this evening in the community center, Bubba has a speaker come in and give a talk on the area we are riding through. I find it quite interesting to know some of the local history. Our speaker describes the region we are riding through and explains the amount of water used from the Colorado River for agriculture. He also mentions how little of this water flows to Mexico.

THE TIME OF MY LIFE

JOURNAL DAY 7

Friday, March 8, 2019

Gila Bend, Arizona to Casa Grande, Arizona

87 miles

Last night when we all entered our tents it was calm in the desert, but what wakes me up at 5 am are gusts of wind that shake my tent violently. I reach for my phone to check the NOAA app and the weather report for the day. I see that the wind will be out of the east in our faces all day long. This is not a good start. Today will be a tough ride for all of us coasters, but as Bubba says, "IT'S ALL GOOD."

At breakfast a few of us discuss how to handle this kind of wind. The general consensus is to take this 87 mile day in 20 mile increments because we are in it for enjoyment. This is not the race across America. Our SAG stops today are at mile markers 28, 42 and 61, so we all say this is doable. The elevation gain is only 1,311 feet for the entire day.

Today's ride is through the Sonoran National Monument land. I look around at the vegetation and the beautiful flowers and it is hard to believe it's still winter. Bubba also mentions at the riders meeting that we will go by a lot of the land that John Wayne owned at one time. Our ride today will also be past a feedlot where thousands of cattle are born and raised for beef in a corral setting. We all know the rest of the story.

Shortly after we pass these feedlots, we come across large rolling hills, and find out later they are huge landfills where refuse from Tucson and Phoenix is deposited. We all know that trash has to go somewhere, but we hate to think it is in the desert.

The long day is coming to an end as we approach the High Chaparral RV Park. Today we pedaled 8 1/2 hours because of strong headwinds.

During our nightly riders meeting, Bubba reviews, in detail, anything else we need to know that was not included in our daily rider sheets. This makes the trip an educational experience. Tonight, Bubba also points out that this is a tour and not a race across America, so take each day in stride.

At our first riders meeting Bubba said, "When you are flying overhead in an airplane, or riding in a car you never see anything up close. When you bike across America you will stop and see the flowers up close, and when you look at the flower up close you may even see the bumble bee." Today during the riders meeting, I walk up to Bubba and look at him square in the eye and I say, "I saw the bumble bee today." Upon hearing that he has a puzzled look on his face and I refresh his memory as to what he said at our first riders meeting. At that moment he remembers and says, "You did huh?" Then Bubba's face turns into a big smile.

This evening I FaceTime with my wife Mary, and tell her I miss her. I have been gone 7 days and this is the longest we have been apart in 34 years. This trip will be the longest time I have been away from Akron, Ohio since my Active Army Training at Ft. Knox, Kentucky in 1971. Where did 48 years go?

JOURNAL DAY 8

Saturday, March 9, 2019

Casa Grande, Arizona to Catalina State Park, Arizona

55 miles

Today is our eighth straight day of riding. As a group of us head out on Battaglia Drive into a low eastern sun, we all look like a row of ducks with our fluorescent vests with our rear lights flashing.

Before I left Mary attached a brim of a hat into my helmet, this served as a great sun visor and worked out well. During these rides I use a 50 spf sunscreen and I am tanning and not burning. This sounds silly, putting suntan lotion on when it was 36 degrees, but it works and feels like it holds the heat in. Last night the temperature dipped down to 36 degrees but it was warm in the tent with no wind. It was so cold I was concerned about my phone so I put my phone inside the sleeping bag.

After going through the breakfast line, it is too cold to eat in the open pavilion, so Bubba has us eat breakfast in the laundry room building of the RV park. At today's end we will have traveled 462 miles from San Diego and what a trip it has been. I am like a kid on Christmas morning, my love for biking and traveling is starting to unfold before me on this trip of a lifetime. Our SAG stop is at the Travel Center at mile 19.

The first half of today is a flat ride, well sort of, except for small hills. Our lunch/ SAG check in is at Nico's Mexican Restaurant at mile marker 36. After lunch we head southeast, then east onto Tangerine Rd. to a very steady uphill grade complete with a slight headwind. This road is straight as an arrow for 15 miles. Zach and I stop to peel off some clothes because the heat index soars to 83 degrees. In Akron, Ohio the high today is supposed to be 27, so no problem here in Arizona.

All of us coasters are instructed to follow the paved bike path that heads into the direction of Catalina State Park. We stop and get a vanilla milkshake at In-N-Out Burger across the street from the park.

Tight Camping

The campground tonight is about a mile off the main road. As we arrive, my eyes are looking for my number 82 tent and it is located on the outer edge of the camping area. What a great view of the mountain range in the park. It islike a picture from a hiking magazine. I lay on my bed and take it all in. Beautiful. We will be camping here 2 straight nights with no riding tomorrow, because this is our first rest day.

There is a phrase Bubba uses, "IT'S ALL GOOD" and after 8 days of riding with no break, up and over mountains, through the Sonoran Desert, Bubba is very positive and his staff is very helpful to all the riders.

At the first rider meeting before our wheel dipping in San Diego, he said he would do everything in his power to get us to St. Augustine, Florida safely. Well after the first week we can all attest that Bubba is a man of his word. Many thanks to you Bubba for all your planning and hard work. Tonight a few of us gather around a campfire and conversation is shared about previous biking adventures. There are always many stories to be told around a campfire.

The Rickus Family Visits

Typical Dinner

Journal Day 9

Sunday, March 10, 2019

Tucson, Arizona

Rest Day

After 8 days of riding over the mountains and in the desert, we are finally looking forward to our first day of rest. We all have plans to get our personal belongings in order, plus cleaning the chains on our bicycles.

Coffee is served at 7:00 and breakfast at 8:00. On rest days our breakfast menu is expanded with more items available. Because today is Sunday we have a short devotional service, led by Beth, one of the SAG support team members. The devotional service lasts about 15 minutes. Whenever Bubba has to leave the tour for any reason, Beth conducts the riders meeting until he returns.

Today a few people have visitors, and I am one of the lucky ones. My niece and nephew Kristin and Bernie and their son, Ryan, (my great nephew) come from Tucson to see me and see how I am doing and what the trip is all about. This is truly a highlight of my trip that they took time out of their busy day to come and see me. They offer to help if I need something from the store and within a few minutes we were standing in a Walmart outside the park. I purchase a bar of soap, sunscreen, Q-tips and a few other incidentals. I want to stock up because I have no idea what lies ahead. Bernie also suggested going to an REI store. Once there I buy electrolyte tablets because little did I know how much I would need them during this ride.

Upon returning to the Catalina State Park, I give them a tour of our encampment where my tent is on the outer edge of the camp with my million dollar view of the Santa Catalina mountain range. Catalina State Park is over 5,000 acres and has many hiking trails throughout the park and into the mountains. The shower facility is almost new. However, we have been warned to keep an eye open for rattlesnakes.

THE TIME OF MY LIFE

Bernie inquires about the route we are taking to Tombstone. He is familiar with the area and mentions the 25 mile climb of 2000 feet we will be doing in 2 days. He said it's a kicker. Considering what we have already done to get this far, it should not be a problem. Ryan is particularly interested because all of us are older adults, averaging 65 years old, a mere 40 years older than him and crossing the country on two wheels. Ryan is gifted with his running abilities. He has earned many medals for his Marathons in Arizona. Before the Rickus family leaves I ask Nancy to take a picture of all of us before we say our goodbyes. This visit was what I needed to pump me up after 8 long days.

I walk back to my tent and gather my riding clothes and items for the next day. I also clean and oil my chain. Most days we all check our tires for any damage and check the air pressure. We always call this "gassing up." Coach, our tour mechanic, always has 6 hand pumps in the "Pampered Zone" for anyone to use.

We have 3 previous C2C coasters join us at dinner, this is always a good time to listen to the stories they have to tell and get a feel for the coming days. A few of us gather around the bonfire as Bubba tells some interesting and funny stories of some of his rides he has experienced over the past 9 years.

We are all winding down and I head back to the tent. I am using a little battery powered light to hang at the peak of the tent so I can see inside the tent. I FaceTime my wife Mary, and she is busy in the basement going through 28 years of stuff and cleaning the house. Then I FaceTime my son Nic, his wife Kristin and my grandchildren Camden and Emory.

Today is a much needed rest day, and I for one needed it after pedaling 8 days straight over the mountains and deserts...flying down Interstate 8. Tonight, will be a cold night in the desert. I use my winter sleeping bag to climb into for the night and I use my summer sleeping bag on top for extra warmth. I take time to post some pictures on Instagram and answer some texts from people who are keeping in touch with me. Most of them are curious about where I am. I also put my phone in my sleeping bag so it won't be frozen in the morning. One of the drawbacks of this camping in the cold night air is having a 1:00 am wake up potty call. I have to walk the length of a football field in the cold night air with a headlamp on.

Journal Day 10

Monday, March 11, 2019

Catalina State Park, Arizona to East Tucson, Arizona

44 Miles

When I wake up this morning it is dark and 41 degrees. Breakfast will be ready in about 30 minutes. I am one of 6 who are headed to get a cup of hot coffee. Zach and John are always the first ones up in the morning and first to get coffee.

Last night we thought the tent would blow away; we had very strong winds up to 20 mph and the sides of the tents were bellowing in and out all night. We all have to hand it to the Wolfpack for setting up fifty-two tents in the windy desert, just hours before we arrived. Our tents are 6 ft 6" tall, with netting on the top dome part of the tent like a shelf. This is a great place to put some light clothing. The floor area is approximately 9 feet square, with pockets on the walls to hold small items. Our air mattresses are inflated 8 inches thick and are then topped off again about 8:00 pm. The girls in the Wolfpack will come around at dark with the Ryobi air pump to make sure the mattress stays full. I always have a flashlight ready when they arrive. Tonight, when things get quiet after dark I call out from inside my tent, "Good night John Boy" and someone else responds, "Goodnight Mary Ellen" and so on, and so on, just like in *The Waltons* tv show. It was funny to hear all the good nights go through numerous tents.

Our luggage is placed inside the tent so when we arrive our duffle bags are available to us. This is being pampered and it doesn't get any better than this. Thank you Wolfpack for all your hard work! This same scenario is repeated in school gymnasiums and National Guard Armories. On hotel nights our luggage is placed in our room. In the morning our responsibility is to take our luggage back to the luggage trailer.

Today our ride will consist mostly of the Tucson Loop Trail. This loop bike trail has over 100 miles of paved trail, and when it is completed it will be 131 miles long. This is one of the premier paved trails in America. Our ride today is from Catalina State Park north of Tucson to the south eastern part of suburban Tucson.

As we ride along we see the largest airplane museum in the world. The airplane graveyard covers hundreds of acres. Airplanes are put here because of the dry climate and wrapped in plastic to preserve any parts that may need recycling.

Tonight we will end up camping at Adventure Bound RV Resort. This will be our last night camping for the next six nights. Most of us are glad to hear that because of the windy, cold desert nights. Today's riding temperature is about 80 degrees and the winds are blowing in all directions, 20-27 mph. We reach camp about 1:00 pm, and the pool looks very inviting, so get out of my way, I'm going for a swim in the pool, this is a treat in the winter months.

Tucson Loop Trail

THE TIME OF MY LIFE

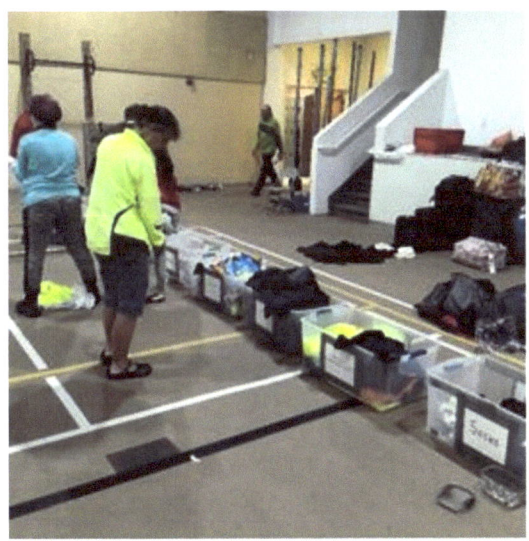

First Laundry Day (DSL)

Journal Day 11

Tuesday, March 12, 2019

East Tucson, Arizona to Tombstone, Arizona

73 miles

Today the forecast is for rain with wind and temperature in the mid 40's. Not a great day for riding across the desert, but once again like Bubba says, "It's all Good."

As we are getting ready to leave, I spot a mountain range 30 some miles away. I mention to the group that we will probably see this same range later this afternoon. Up, up we go into the Santa Rita Mountain Range. We gain 2,000 feet in 25 miles of pedaling. We know this day is going to be a long one because of the swirling winds and the 3,861 feet of altitude gain over the entire day. Late in the morning we have rain that turns to sleet as we gain altitude. We are already getting cold; my feet are freezing and we all just keep pedaling and thinking about the nice hotel we will be in tonight with hot showers and a warm bed.

We have two SAG stops today, mile 23 and 55. Our lunch is in a quaint little place called The Cafe, on AZ-82, just east of Sonoita, Arizona where we all take time to eat, relax and dry out a bit before venturing on. It is a cold, windy day. The landscape changes from low desert to Saguaro Cacti with a lot of tumbleweed. These tumbleweeds have goat-head thorns on them that can penetrate a tire. We are told to try to avoid them if possible, even when parking the bike. Always double check tires before riding again.

We arrive at the hotel for the night around 4 pm and can still see the mountain range that we saw this morning when we started. The hotel name is the Landmark Lookout Lodge. It was built on a hillside and overlooks the high desert valley.

THE TIME OF MY LIFE

Tonight I will be rooming with retired U.S. Air Force, Lt. Colonel John S. John loves to tell stories about his military and civilian life. He is a good storyteller and keeps everyone laughing with his great sense of humor.

At the riders meeting we are informed that the DSL will be collected outside the hotel office in the morning. There are about 9 laundry baskets and they're all labeled on what should be in it. Weeks before this tour we were asked to pick a number. To keep laundry separate for 43 riders, we all labeled our clothing, socks, underwear, biking clothes with a name or a specific #. I chose number 42 because, when I was a kid I used to ask my dad for answers and if he didn't know, he would tell me 42. So all my belongings are marked with #42. The SAG team washes, dries and folds our clothes and we have them back on the same day. It is our responsibility to pick them up. If you do not pick them up by the time of the rider meeting, Bubba will slightly embarrass you and make an entertaining show of your laundry, complete with jokes.

It's a good thing we are in a hotel tonight.... because outside it's a cold one.

The Continental Divide

JOURNAL DAY 12

Wednesday, March 13, 2019

Tombstone, Arizona to Douglas, Arizona

50 miles

It was a good thing we stayed at the Landmark Lookout Lodge last night because all 43 of us knew the start of this day was going to be a cold and windy ride. The day begins in the upper 30's. Riding through downtown Tombstone, it looks more like a ghost town because not too many people are out at this time of day.

As we pedal this morning, to the southwest of us is San Pedro Riparian National Conservation Area and the Fort Huachuca Army Post. We all know a few miles ahead of us we will encounter some uphill grades of up to 7%. The positive side of this is that we will be creating our own body heat. Up and up we go and, in the distance, we can see the mountains have a fresh coat of snow on them. Reaching the Continental Divide at 6,030 feet, we all stop at the obelisk marking the Divide. We take pictures and make snowballs like a bunch of school children. This is the highest elevation on our entire tour and we conquered it!

Next starts a series of switchbacks down the mountain, we are on the lookout for black ice, also watching our speed due to the steep grade. This ride will be almost 3 miles and this is the coldest I have ever been on a bicycle. The positive outlook is that our lunch stop is at The High Desert Cafe in Bisbee. Zach and I both order the meatloaf and endless cups of hot coffee. It appears by the crowd, the whole group turned this lunch break into an hour and a half to recoup our body heat. Downtown Bisbee is an artsy, crafty southwestern town. Everyone is dressed in western wear, cowboy boots and hats. Bubba suggests we stop at the Bisbee Bicycle Brothel on Main St. This is a very interesting shop with a huge display of antique bicycles, parts

The Copper Queen Mine

and accessories, it is like a museum. I browse around and buy a ball cap with the name of the store on it as a souvenir. Riding another mile, we all stop at the Copper Queen Mine and take pictures. This mine is 900 feet in depth and a mile across. It closed to copper mining in 1975 and is now a tourist attraction.

Moving forward on our journey we pick up AZ-80E and we are back into the desert. The road is straight for many, many miles with no buildings, houses, ranches, cell towers, absolutely nothing to be seen. This is the point where I start singing out loud, "America the Beautiful." Also I pick another song, "A Horse with No Name," sung by America. Song written by Dewey and released in late 1971. Dewey was the lead vocalist and acoustic guitar player of the group. The song is a certified gold record.

After a while you don't even give a thought to pedaling. It just becomes second nature and you and the bike are one. The majority of the 25 miles into Douglas is a pleasant ride with the sun shining. And, we finally have a tailwind that helps push us into our night's stay.

Upon arriving in Douglas, AZ we are all told to go to the Gadsden Hotel. The hotel is on the National Registry of Historic places. We are informed as to whether we will stay here or at the Best Western Hotel. For lack of accommodations for the full group, Bubba has the couples and the crew stay at the historic Gadsden with Tiffany glass and marble staircase. Within walking distance most of us bachelors, or single riders, myself included, will stay in the Best Western which is 1/3 of a mile from the Mexican border.

This evening for dinner Bubba gives our culinary team, Anne and Serge the night off. This gives a few of us the opportunity to tour this famous hotel and to eat dinner at the Gadsden Hotel Restaurant. I have a steak and baked potato, salad and veggies. During the tour we learn about the folklore story of Poncho Villa, the Robin Hood of his day. He rode his horse up the marble staircase and there is a big chip out of the seventh marble step they claim was made by the horse's hoof.

We take a group picture of the 2019 Coast to Coast tour on this famous marble staircase. For all the movie buffs, there were some famous western movies filmed here. *The Life and Times of Judge Roy Bean* with Paul Newman. *Ruby Jean and Joe* with Tom Selleck. Filmed in the bar was *Terminal Velocity* with Charlie Sheen.

After dinner we have our regular riders meeting, then we pick up our clean laundry. Today was just a long cold day with 2,416 ft of elevation up and over the Huachuca Mountains, but as the saying goes..... IT'S ALL GOOD.

Journal Day 13

Thursday, March 14, 2019

Douglas, Arizona to Rodeo, New Mexico

55 miles

Today's ride is only 55 miles with 1,247 feet of elevation gain. Those of us who stayed at the Best Western (which is 6 blocks away) have to meet up with the other half of the group who are at the Gadsden Hotel where we will all eat the breakfast buffet together. After breakfast, we pick up our clean laundry in the meeting room.

By this point in the trip, the whole group is getting comfortable with our daily routine. We are getting to know each other and our different traits. I realize our main focus is to ride across the country and make new lifelong friends.

The next few days we will be riding in desolate territory with no towns in between. When we check our weather conditions, it looks like we are going to have a break from the wind today and it will be in our favor.

At the riders meeting last night both Bubba and Coach reminded us to watch for the Goathead thorns in the bushy areas where we may have parked our bikes. Before starting out we are to spin our tires and double check to make sure none stuck to them.

A SAG Stop With Zach

Riding along AZ-80 East we enjoy the view of the miles of snowcapped Chiricahua Mountains. I stop several times to take pictures as the riders go by. Because we are not going through any towns, our lunch SAG stop today is at mile marker 40. This is an historical marker where Apache Indian Chief Geronimo, surrendered in 1886 to our US ARMY

At mile marker 54 we are about a mile from camp and several of us stop at the Chiricahua Desert Museum and browse around to see items that survive in the desert, such as plants, animals and reptiles.

Today's ride is somewhat short due to the tailwind. Upon arriving at the Chiricahua Mountain Lodge, we are assigned our sleeping accommodations either at the Lodge or the Painted Pony Resort 3 miles away. I was assigned to sleep at the Lodge. This resort was built by John McAfee. It is a 756 acre high desert Estate with a pool, hot tub, games, and other amenities. It has a total of 5 buildings, including an airplane hangar. The Estate is 7,000 sq. ft. Sleeps 40, has 10 bedrooms, 7 bathrooms, one half bath and there is a minimum 2 night stay. It is advertised as "An Escape to Tranquil Beauty." This was built for hang gliding enthusiasts, but it is also used for family reunions, weddings, workshops, conferences, stargazing and a Getaway Place. We all eat dinner together and tomorrow morning we will eat breakfast at the Painted Pony Ranch.

After dinner, Bubba has a speaker come in and talk about the geology of the region. He also reminds us we have been pedaling in the Gadsden Purchase since we left Arizona. This land was purchased by the United States from Mexico in 1853 for the sum of 10 million dollars. The purchase was named after James Gadsden who was America's Ambassador to Mexico. A few years later the railroad came through here and started laying track

Anne's Mobile Kitchen

Journal Day 14

Friday, March 15, 2019

Rodeo, New Mexico to Columbus, New Mexico

92 miles

Waking up this cold dark morning we are shuttled from the Chiricahua Mountain Lodge to the Painted Pony Ranch about 3 miles away where we eat breakfast. We make our sandwiches to gear up with nutrition for the day. Once again, we will ride all day long without passing through any towns. Heading east into the sun we currently have no wind. Around Mid-Morning the wind kicks up. The gusts of wind are blowing in three directions, sometimes it feels like it is going to blow you over. Some of the guys refer to these circular winds as DUST DEVILS, like a mini tornado. Today the 1,804 feet of elevation gain seems a lot harder because of the swirling winds.

All of our breakfasts and dinners are prepared by Anne, the chef, and her husband Serge from Culinary Insider. They drive two trucks, one is the mobile kitchen and one is their motorhome. The food she prepares for us is excellent quality. Ann bakes for us along the way and also prepares vegan dishes.

Today our ride will take us along the Mexican border. Border Patrol Agents are busy dragging the sandy road that runs parallel to the road we are pedaling on. The purpose of dragging is to pick up the fresh footprints of anyone trying to cross the border illegally. We are crossing over our second Continental Divide which is not as steep as the last one, this is a more gradual grade. Today the chill factor is making it a very, very cold ride due to the wind. I put on my bright yellow rain shell as a windbreak, gloves, and a stocking cap.

Several of us make a stop on the side of the road and I comment, "I would give $10 for a cup of hot coffee." A couple of the riders laugh and say they would pay that also. Today's ride is one of those days where you just want to finish the ride and forget about it.

THE TIME OF MY LIFE

Today I take a short walk in the desert. I need to regroup mentally on this 3,000 mile ride. When riding in the open desert, there is nothing at all but wide open spaces. You have plenty of time to pray and sing. Bubba has commented that former coasters have contacted him from the previous 9 years of C2C trips saying this year by far has been the toughest year because of the weather conditions we have to deal with every day.

For the ten years Bubba has been doing this tour he has posted a few pictures on Facebook, of each year's ride so previous coasters can relive that dream. It also lets followers check on friends and family members and of course, there is some advertising for his tour.

Tomorrow is our second rest day of the bike tour. We are staying at the New Mexico, Columbus Elementary School gymnasium and taking all of our 5 meals in the school cafeteria, provided by the school cafeteria staff. It is the weekend, there are no students around. Our bedroom tonight is a 90 x 120 ft. gym where all 56 air mattresses are spaced out in rows on the basketball court floor. Our bicycles are wheeled in for the night and parked wherever we can lean them up on a wall or bleacher.

At 8:50 pm, when we stay in a gymnasium or armory, Coach announces, we have 10 minutes to get settled before lights out. Coach, our bike mechanic is in charge of the lights out at 9:00 pm every night.

Coach was a high school track coach in Michigan and that's how he got his name. He is a tall man and very sociable. He likes to tell stories of his experiences in life as a farmer and a teacher. In his spare time (ha ha) Coach and his son run a bike shop. He is very accommodating and helpful to all of us when it comes to a mechanical or tire issue on the bikes. Thanks Coach!

Journal Day 15

Saturday, March 16, 2019

Columbus, New Mexico

Rest day

After a very restful sleep we all file into the cafeteria at 8:00 am while the school cafeteria staff makes us a full breakfast. We thank them many times over for getting up so early on their day off.

Today is a dreary, cool rainy day; to keep busy a lot of us clean and oil our chains. At 10 am for all of those interested, we are shuttled to the Pancho Villa Museum in the Pancho Villa State Park. Most everyone agrees on the offer to explore and see something new, a historian gives a small presentation on the area we are in.

Poncho Villa would rob primarily businesses with his soldiers, sometimes killing soldiers and civilians. On one raid in Columbus, New Mexico he killed 8 soldiers and 10 civilians. In later years of his life, Villa was in his 1919 Dodge Roadster with four of his bodyguards and someone shouted "VIVA VILLA!" As the story goes, seven riflemen appeared and fired more than forty bullets into the car, nine bullets went into his head. Poncho died immediately. His body was found with his hand reaching for his gun. He died in 1923 at the age of 45.

Lunch in Mexico

After leaving the museum we travel about 2 miles to the US/Mexico border where we all walk across the border to Puerto Paloma's in Mexico. We have lunch at the Pink Store and the first Margarita is on the house. We enjoy a trio of singers and their guitars moving from table to table. After lunch we all wander through the Pink Store gift shop, and I purchase Mary a pair of silver earrings. After leaving the Pink Store, we gather across the street in front of the Poncho Villa statue for a group picture. Staying together as a group, we head through customs at the border with just our driver's license or passport.

When we arrive back to the school, it appears all of us have something to do to get ready for the next day's ride, even if it is just to organize our personal belongings or take a well- deserved nap.

In celebration of St Patrick's Day, the Mexican cafeteria staff makes us Corned Beef and Cabbage for the Irish dinner and they do a darn good job! During our dessert we had our riders meeting and Bubba mentions tonight will be our last night in New Mexico. Tomorrow will begin our first of 19 nights in Texas and well over 1,000 riding miles in Texas alone. Like all school and National Guard Armory nights, all the main lighting will be out at 9 pm, thanks to Coach. There are some of us who continue to text, email or download pictures to Instagram and Facebook for all followers to see.

This is our second rest day and I made one rule to follow that is important. Mandatory........NO bike riding on rest days!!

Journal Day 16

Sunday, March 17, 2019

Columbus, New Mexico to El Paso, Texas

75 miles

All of us enjoyed our day off even if the weather didn't cooperate. Like Bubba says, "It's all Good!" Today being Sunday, we have our weekly non-denominational devotion service led by Beth. There are about 12-14 in attendance. Beth has a very even tone and calming voice. She starts with a couple scripture readings, followed by a short talk. She challenges us to reach out to four other people this week in the group and ask them something about themselves. This short service really helps us get through the week and motivates us to get to know each other better.

As we roll out of the Columbus Elementary School about 8 am and head east into the sun, the temperature is in the upper 40s and we all came dressed for the cooler weather. We turn onto New Mexico R-9 East, the sun is directly in our eyes.

We pedal past an old Army Airfield from 1916 that was used by the Aviation Signal Corp as an airfield during the Poncho Villa era. The airfield was closed and abandoned in the late 1970s and today efforts are being made to re-establish it as a general aviation site.

While pedaling in the desert we see memorials or small shrines on the side of the road for victims of car accidents.

Many are very elaborate with names, dates, flowers, pictures and rosaries.

Pedaling along we have a headwind blowing directly at us, at about 10 mph. We are getting used to the wind being in our face, but as you all know the wind usually blows from west to east so this wind will change throughout the day.

THE TIME OF MY LIFE

Today's lunch is at mile marker 48, Bubba provides us with an assortment of Subway sandwiches the SAG team has picked up, because once again we are not passing through any towns. All day today we are pedaling parallel to the Mexican border, anywhere within one to four miles of the line. The good news is we have 826 ft of elevation and 1,248 ft of descent, in Bubba's language "this is HUGE!"

As Zach and I get closer to El Paso there are many industrial sites that are located on both sides of the highway. After making a couple left and right turns we came down a hill and at the bottom there is a bridge with the Rio Grande River flowing beneath us. We stop at the bridge to take pictures. The River is 80% dried up. The water is being dispersed for agricultural use in the United States and not much water is going to Mexico.

With only two miles to go, we stop at McDonalds to get some ice cream. Today the weather is in the low 80's with a sidewind of 7-8 mph.

We arrive at the Quality Inn for our night's stay around 4:00. Anne has hot chili cheese dip, nachos and assorted crackers and cheese. I walk into the lobby and look for Snowflake; she is responsible for distributing the room keys. I retrieve my room key and go to my room for a quick shower and to relax a bit before dinner at 6 pm. For dinner we have pesto chicken, baked sweet potato, quinoa and homemade Ratatouille, garden salad and Haagen Daz ice cream bars for dessert.

At the riders meeting, Bubba warns us about sitting under the Mesquite trees in the evening. He said be very careful not to disturb anything. Everyone looks puzzled and wants to know why. Bubba says, "Just when you least expect it .... the mosquitoes will come out." Ha ha (Another Bubba Joke)

Bubba has a few rules to follow so everyone has a good time. One thing he requests is that we refrain from talking about politics, religion and sex. These 3 subjects seem to get some adults in trouble as a rule. All of us agree to this simple task.

THE TIME OF MY LIFE

JOURNAL DAY 17

Monday, March 18, 2019

El Paso, Texas to Fort Hancock, Texas

61 miles

The Quality Inn supplies us with a full breakfast this morning, this allows Anne and Serge some time off, so they can jump ahead for tonight's stay at Fort Hancock, some 61 miles to the south/east.

The riders sheet today has many left and right turns, and directs us through a residential neighborhood. Bubba recommends at the riders meeting to stop at a point of interest that looks out over the city of El Paso and Ciudad Juarez Mexico. This is one of 4 border crossings in El Paso, into Mexico, and the most famous one is the Bridge of the Americas. Within the first 8 miles of the day we have 11 turns.

A couple miles to our northeast is Fort Bliss, which is the home of the first armored tank division. Our first SAG stop is at mile marker 19.7 and after our check in, we walk into the Latino supermarket named El Supermarket. Last night at the riders meeting Bubba gave us another tip to look for in the market, and that is the bakery section where we can sit and rest for a while. I believe every rider decides to stop in the bakery for something sweet to eat. After our sweet treat, we all walk around the store observing different products because most everything is written in Spanish. This market is very similar to our Acme or Giant Eagle. While walking through the store it is easy to spot each other because we all have on our bright fluorescent safety vests.

Slowly, leaving the urban area of El Paso and connecting to RT-20, we ride along the border fence that separates us from Mexico. The road is nicely paved but we still have those pesky headwinds to contend with. Bubba also warns us about the hundreds of acres of pecan groves we pass, Bubba emphasized, "DO NOT PICK ANY!"

Riding through the pecan groves I think about where these nuts will end up. Later, we find out why the pecan groves are plowed. It is to let the water reach the roots easier through the loose soil.

Many of the homes and ranches are very close to the road so we are always on the lookout for dogs running loose, and today we hit the lottery. We have three pesky dogs, the first is a barking Chihuahua. The second dog that chases us is a Heinz 57 mixed breed who is a little bigger. The third is fast and difficult to outpedal because he is out for an ankle; he looks like a pit bull. We are instructed early on to speak firmly to the dogs, tell them no and they will usually back away. But the pit bull gives me a run for my money. I shift 2 gears feeling like Mario Andretti and thank God the dog gives up before I do.

Finally, we arrive at our lunch check in at mile 37. El Fredo's is a Mexican style restaurant. After two weeks I am getting my fill of Mexican food, so I order a cheeseburger with onion rings and drink two cups of hot coffee, just to warm up my hands. With 24 miles left in the day we head down a slight grade and the winds for some reason almost stop.

Tonight's stay is at Fort Hancock High School. For all you movie buffs, this is the town where Morgan Freeman and Tim Robbins crossed over to Mexico in the movie, *The Shawshank Redemption.* This movie was partly filmed at the old Mansfield Reformatory in Mansfield, Ohio which is now a permanently closed prison, but is open for tours. It was also filmed in parts of downtown Ashland, and Mansfield, Ohio.

While pedaling through these vast wide open spaces, sometimes you hear some riders singing and two of our riders are listening to music.

The Sisters of St. Dominic at Our Lady of the Elms in Akron, Ohio offered to say prayers daily for a safe journey for all of us riders pedaling across the United States. For their prayers, I am grateful. Thank you Sisters. Some are also the teachers that taught me in grade school.

THE TIME OF MY LIFE

Of all the days crossing the country, we never miss a hot shower and you may be wondering if we had to take our own towels. You have to remember this is a Pampered tour and Bubba provides microfiber washcloths and towels on all nights except for the nights we stay in hotels. Yes, we are all spoiled. Tonight's meal consists of Braised Beef, salad, rice, mixed vegetables and chocolate pecan pie. Tomorrow morning we will eat our breakfast in the same place as dinner, about 250 yards from the school at the Fort Hancock Community Church meeting room. The church and school are located one mile from Mexico.

The Rio Grande River

Puerto Paloma's in Mexico

Journal Day 18

Tuesday, March 19, 2019

Fort Hancock, Texas to Van Horn, Texas

74 miles

We awake to warmer temperatures. I can't believe it's still winter according to the calendar. We are still headed east and the sun is still shining in our eyes on Texas Rt-20 E, for our first 21 miles. Our first SAG stop of the day is at the Drivers Travel Mart.

When we enter Interstate 10 E, we notice that the speed limit is 80 mph. Most of us coasters actually feel comfortable riding on a superhighway for two reasons, the first is the smooth pavement on the wide berms (other than the rumble strips). You do still have to watch for the debris though. Second, the road grade is no more than 7%. However, when semi-trucks start to pass us, it feels like the air sucks you in and when the truck passes then it releases that vacuum and the bike jerks the other way. You have to be on your guard at all times.

We travel Interstate 10 for two miles, we cross over into the central time zone and shortly after that we run into a construction site. With gravel in our way, we walk our bikes to the frontage road that runs parallel to Interstate 10. The frontage road continues eastward.

West of Van Horn we pass a talc factory. Talc is actually talcum, a mineral mined from rocks, which is baby powder. It also is a thickening agent in lubricants, an ingredient in ceramics, paint, roofing materials and is also the main ingredient in many cosmetic products.

We keep checking our tires for the goat head thorns. I look at the back tire and it is clear. Checking the front tire, I notice there is a thorn, which I pull out. You have to use a glove because they are thorny and are stiff enough to puncture a tire. Checking the tire will hopefully prevent me from getting a flat on the road.

THE TIME OF MY LIFE

The Davis Mountain Range is to the north of us, it is named after the secretary of war and later Confederate President Jefferson Davis. The highest peak in the range is Mt. Livermore at 8,383 ft. It lies between mile markers 23 and 30. We have a 1,000 ft elevation climb.

Cruising along this particular day, we pass a gas station and a motel that are abandoned. I stop to talk to one of the locals about this and their answer is, once the interstate was built a lot of people stopped going through the small towns. We spoke to the high school kids, they tell us that after graduation most leave town for jobs, go to college or join the military. Each year the towns get smaller and smaller.

At mile marker 41 our SAG lunch stop is at Delfina's Restaurant in Sierra Blanca. This is the second time on this trip I go for a walk by myself to regroup mentally. This is really a tough day. The wind is stepping on my last nerve. We are required to stop and check in with someone, but are not required to eat at the SAG check ins.

Riding another 19 miles we have our third SAG stop of the day and then back onto Rt-10 for eight more miles. Around 3 pm, I arrive at exit 138 and find our campground, Van Horn RV Park is just 3 miles away.

Four of us are riding together today, and one rider by the name of Mike B. who is riding behind me, notices that my rear tire is low. We all stop and examine the tire. I realize there is a small wire that has penetrated both the tire and the tube of the Continental Four Season Vectran tire. These tires run about $90 a tire. Mike uses tweezers and pulls it out, then a SAG member by the name of Frances pulls up beside us and hands me an air pump out the vehicle window. The first pump up gets me about a 1/4 mile and then Frances comes up again and hands me the pump to get me through the last 1/4 mile to camp. Thank you, Frances, and the 3 other riders for following me in and not leaving me stranded on the side of the road. I must have an angel on my shoulder because after spotting my tent, I notice that Coach has his mobile bike shop set up 28 ft from my tent.

Coach sees my dilemma and says, "just bring it over and I will get to it within the hour." He says, "go and relax, you had a long day on the road." I reply with "Thanks Coach I really appreciate you." I see Taco from the Wolfpack and ask him if the bike parts trailer is accessible. I have a flat and need an extra tube out of my parts bag for Coach. It never fails, whenever there is an issue with something, it is worked out one way or another. No worries for anything.

JOURNAL DAY 19

Wednesday, March 20, 2019

Van Horn, Texas to Marfa, Texas

73 miles

Last night was a cold night in our tents, but I had a good night's sleep. Before I dress and get out of the sleeping bag, I check the temperature on my phone and it is currently a balmy 36 degrees with frost on our tents. I quickly dress and head out for coffee as usual. It isn't long before Anne calls us to breakfast. Due to the chilly weather, Bubba suggests we all go to the RV Park laundry room (where it is warm) to eat our breakfast, the laundry room is 20x30. Bubba also manages to squeeze in the riders meeting there this morning, good move, because it was too cold last night to have it in the pavilion.

Today is a long day, from mile marker 10 to mile 55 is a steady uphill grade. We gain 1,246 ft, with many rolling hills. We check the weather and find out we will have headwinds for most of the day. Oh well, as Bubba always says, "It's all good."

One thing I do notice is that there is no complaining among us. We all knew from the start what the program is and we have to handle what comes our way. I, for one, am thrilled to do a trip like this and see our country from sea to sea. This trip is a great experience meeting all new friends and locals that cross our path.

Today we will ride entirely on Rt- 90 East, so it is next to impossible for any of us senior citizens to get lost. It has been days since we saw any trees, so this presents a small problem. Two of the coasters relieve themselves and are caught by Constable Garcia. After tracking Bubba down, Constable Garcia has a talk with Bubba and says, "Tell your riders to go farther away from the road, so the vehicles passing by can't see as well."

CLARENCE BECHTER

We are in the middle of nowhere in Texas and come across a Prada store complete with a window display of shoes and purses. We find out this was put in by the Art Production Fund. The building itself is about 25 x 25 feet and is not actually a store but it is amusing to us coasters.

As we pedal across the states, you will never believe what is laying on the sides of the road. There are nails, screws, wires, glass, coins, tools and, oh yeah, we even see license plates. These plates are the treasures Zach picks up for his collection of state plates.

This is the second day of 19 days crossing the state of Texas, from El Paso to the Sabine River on the border of Louisiana. Texas totals 1,087 miles, and will consist of 33% of our trip.

Our lunch stop is in Valentine, Texas at the K Johnson Memorial Library. Around the back of the building, the high school students are making us tacos and burritos. It is a fundraiser for their class. Once again Bubba introduces every student and has them say what they have in mind for their future plans. All eight students are going on to college after they graduate. Lunch consisted of two burritos, a brownie and a bottle of water. We eat on long tables and the kids put out a grassy mat so everything is green and clean. After lunch we walk in the library and browse. This library is no bigger than a double car garage.

As we head down Rt-90 we see a huge white blimp about 80 ft long set back off the road; this is nicknamed the Spy Station. This blimp is tethered off the ground with cameras on it to detect illegals attempting to cross the border.

Today is a full 8 hour day in the saddle, and at one point the wind changes direction and gives us a break for about 15 miles. We pedal past the western edge of the Ryan Ranch and riding for 10 more miles we pass the eastern end of the Ryan Ranch. I figured the Ranch was about 1/2 the size of Summit County, in Ohio.

Just before reaching the Marfa Activity Center, there is a Dairy Queen that Bubba suggests we stop at. After we order our cold treats, the girl behind the counter says, "No charge, some guy by the name of Bubba paid for it." We reach the Marfa Activity Center, a big gymnasium, 1/4 mile away around 4 pm. Anne has the snacks set out for us and a Border Patrol Officer is here to welcome us into town. We all get organized, take a shower and relax. After dinner we go outside to see the full moon rising in the eastern sky.

After a long day we all are snug in our sleeping bags, ready to drop off for a restful night's sleep, when suddenly out of nowhere, an Amtrak train comes roaring through town, blowing his whistle about 90 feet away from our accommodations.

Windy Day

Journal Day 20

Thursday, March 21, 2019

Marfa, Texas to Marathon, Texas

57 miles

Last night before going to bed I set my alarm for 5:59 am. And you may be thinking why not 6:00? I guess it just sounds better. I am already up when the alarm goes off. On my way to get some coffee, I come across a small group of coasters, they are already on their second cup. The topic of conversation most mornings is the NOAA weather app. This is the abbreviation for the National Oceanic Atmospheric Administration. We find this is one of the most accurate weather apps to follow and check it frequently. The conclusion after our brief meeting is… just deal with whatever comes along. After a while it became a humorous exercise we would all participate in before breakfast.

Last night at the riders meeting Bubba mentioned that for safety reasons, to start the day out, we would ride west toward the start of our trip. But we would only ride west for a quarter mile to pick up the main road, then turn east into a low sun. Bubba had it marked on our riders paper that while riding east on US-90 this morning the sun would be directly in the drivers eyes making it difficult for bicyclists to be seen. It was recommended that we stay off the road from 8:00 to 8:30 as this is the worst time.

At mile marker 9 we come to a rest area for the viewing of the Marfa Lights. The Marfa Lights are a desert phenomenon. Looking out at the desert in the dark if you are lucky you may be able to see the colored lights flash across the sky. These lights have been here for thousands of years. Scientists are still puzzled about the origin of this laser type display.

At mile marker 26.8 in Alpine, it is lunchtime and Bubba suggests we go to the Bread and Breakfast Bakery Cafe. They have great sandwiches and a cinnamon roll to die for. Once inside the smells are wonderful and I have a blueberry muffin and a glass of chocolate milk. Reminiscing for a moment, I think back to being a kid, a 20 mile biking day was HUGE. Alpine also has an Amtrak station which Mary and I plan to visit in the future.

From the start of the trip, Bubba has encouraged us to speak to locals by asking them what type of job they have or had. To start any conversation, this is a great way to get a feel for people who live in small towns that may be 60 miles from the next town. Many times, they will bring up historical facts about the town, the area, border skirmishes or tell us about some movies that were filmed in the area.

As we ride through these small towns every day, something comes to my attention. Just about every town has a dollar store, also a Family Dollar that has a gasoline station. There is no doubt that these stores have taken the place of the Mom and Pop stores that used to be on every corner. I guess sometimes you have to go with the flow and quit trying to swim upstream.

Some days you pedal and don't even know it, it has become second nature. It was times like this that the song "America the Beautiful" comes to mind. This is my theme song for the trip because we are looking at the purple mountains majesty and all the fruited plains and of course from sea to shining sea.

Journal Day 21

Friday, March 22, 2019

Marathon, Texas

Rest Day

This is our first of two nights camping at Marathon RV Park which is about 3/4 miles west of Marathon at an elevation of 4,055 ft. The climate is considered semi-arid with average high temps for March around 70 and the average low around 35. This RV park has about a dozen cabins, so the staff and the married couples are assigned to the cabins. For the tent campers, the good news is we can use a few of the select cabins to take our showers in, which turns out to be a great idea. The only minor glitch is that our tents are set up about 200 yards away from the cabins and our eating area. But it's fine, it gives us a chance to stretch our legs.

About half of the coasters choose to go with Bubba to Big Bend National Park which is about 3 hours away. Today will be a relaxing day for the rest of us who chose not to go with Bubba. Several of us who stayed at camp walk to town to grab a coffee and a snack. We stop to do some shopping for Halls cough drops, some Vitamins C and some cough medicine, just to be prepared. I do not want my immune system to wear down. We have a few coasters with colds and coughing, but nothing serious. Sherry missed a few days on our second week where she took a few SAG rides, but she is back riding daily.

We visit the historic Gage Hotel while we are in town to check it out. It is refurbished in a southwest design. When traveling through this way again I will stay at the Gage Hotel. The others walk back to camp and I stay in town to explore some more. I find St. Mary's Catholic Church, stop in and say a few prayers, and thank God for the safe journey on this adventurous trip.

THE TIME OF MY LIFE

Lunch time is coming so I walk back to camp. Anne has a nice lunch ready for us of different cheeses, meats, potato salad, and chips. After lunch I walk back to my tent, I have time to clean and oil my bike chain, check my tire pressure which I do about every other day. I just do what I see the others doing because some of them have been on this tour before. After I complete my tasks, I take a 30 minute power nap. When I wake up I check the temperature and it is 74 degrees and sunny. Life Is Good!

I try to post some pictures on Instagram and realize something has happened that I cannot figure out. I walk over to the Pampered Zone, there are a few coasters relaxing. I tell Sherry a little about my dilemma. Sherry takes my phone and closes my Instagram app and loads it again, and suddenly it is working. This is what I use to post my pictures daily so friends and family can follow me. Many thanks to Sherry for fixing my Instagram. I walk back to town by myself to the coffee shop for another cup of coffee around 2:30. I go to the ATM Machine to get some extra cash and for some reason the card or process does not work. Then I call the bank to find out the issue, evidentially I entered the wrong password.

Anytime Bubba or any of us see a self-contained rider, Bubba encourages us to invite them into our camp for the evening. These riders are treated to one of Anne's nice hot dinners, breakfast in the morning and a hot shower before they ride away. The only catch is that they have to give a short presentation to the group about their travels. On this particular night Bubba invites a self-contained couple into our camp. They are from England and in their late 20's and are pedaling across the United States, self-contained on a Tandem bike. In their presentation they tell us they sold everything they had owned and took off. They are taking side trips and figure it may take them about three months. This type of adventure takes a lot of guts, but think of the rewards and the time of their life they will have together. It will be well worth it. They will be able to tell stories to their children and grandchildren. After the presentation, we have a riders meeting in the open air pavilion. The sun is going down quickly and so is the temperature. I walk back to my tent and FaceTime Mary, it is difficult for her to hear me because of the wind. She can hear the sides of the tent flapping. This wind is so loud I have to insert my ear plugs in order to get some sleep. I wear a headlamp to read a little before turning in for the night. As I read I can feel the temperature drop. I get up and put on an extra jacket, my stocking cap and put my extra sleeping bag on top of me. Now I am cozy and warm as I turn out the light.

Bubba and Two British Riders

THE TIME OF MY LIFE

JOURNAL DAY 22

Saturday, March 23, 2019

Marathon, Texas to Sanderson, Texas

56 miles

I wake up in the dark about 6:00 am to go get coffee. I have to walk about 200 yards and noticeably the winds have calmed down. Today our ride is relatively short and all day we will ride on US-90. It is an uphill ride that will give us 742 feet in elevation gain. But the good news is the last 36 miles of the day is all downhill for a decline of 2,008 feet.

Today is another perfect day to ride, I make the time to stop and take pictures and there is absolutely nothing around. The wind is no longer blowing, you can almost hear your heartbeat. Today's ride will only take us four hours and we will be finished for the day. We cannot believe we are already at our destination and it is noon.

Bubba suggests lunch at the Ranch House which is one mile past our overnight accommodations at Sanderson High School. For lunch I order Texas Beef Brisket. As I am ordering I notice all the waitresses are wearing a holstered sidearm. I decide at this point, I should not complain about my service or my food. LOL. The town of Sanderson is known as the Cactus capital of Texas. For all you movie buffs, the movie *No Country for Old Men* was filmed in Sanderson and Del Rio Texas areas.

Most towns we pass through have one magnificent structure in town and that is the courthouse. The Terrell county courthouse across from where we are staying is also a showpiece. It has a memorial park in the front. Across from the courthouse, is St. James Catholic Church. I stop at the church for a visit and a few prayers, once again I express my thankfulness for a safe adventure. Today, just before dinner I call Bob at Falls Wheel and Wrench bicycle shop in Cuyahoga Falls, Ohio and talk to him about the trip so far. He is living his dream through me. Bob is a business man and cannot take the time for a coast to coast ride. I purchased my Jamis Renegade Bicycle from him.

At dinner tonight, we have beef brisket and ironically the same fellow that cooked for us at the Ranch House at lunch time also cooks the beef brisket for dinner. The Sanderson High School students serve us dinner, and top it off with cake and pie for desert. Bubba does mention that there is a tip jar to help these students with school trips.

Bubba has four self-contained riders, all with British backgrounds, for an overnight stay, with 2 meals. After dinner they entertain us with short presentations on where they are going and why. The first two riders are Lloyd and Lewis, emergency room doctors, who are raising money for Spinal Research and the Brain Foundation and are on a trek to pedal their tandem bike around the world. Later in their presentation they tell us that this trip is also to establish them in the Guinness Book of World Records for fastest circumnavigation by tandem bicycle (male). I am curious about their travels so I talk with them for about 5 minutes, and take their picture. I have stayed in contact with Lloyd since meeting them in Sanderson, Texas.

The duo started pedaling on August 7, 2018, in Adelaide, South Australia. They completed their entire journey in 9 months, on May 16, 2019. They pedaled more than 18,000 miles. In November 2019 they were informed they surpassed the previous held record by 9 days. Congratulations Doctors, job well done!!

The second couple of self-contained riders are British with very strong British accents. They are in their mid 50's and very hard to understand at times. Their presentation is like a rehearsed comedy act which is quite amusing, these two riders are pedaling across the United States for something to do.

On the mornings when we stay in a school gym or National Guard setting, Papow, one of our SAG team members, plays soft, upbeat music to get the troops moving. The music he plays is very good for our age group, from the Beatles to Herman's Hermits and about every 10 minutes the volume increases just a little. That is a nice way to get everyone awake. Thanks, Papow.

Journal Day 23

Sunday, March 24, 2019

Sanderson, Texas to Comstock, Texas

82 miles

Last night was a good night to sleep, the temperatures were in the mid 60's and one of the gym doors was open for air. It is a hoot to sleep with sixty people in one large setting. It is incredibly interesting just observing how everyone gets ready for bed and rises in the morning for another day's adventure. Papow's instrumental music helps to get the crowd moving again this morning. He is an enjoyable person to know, partly due to his mismatched socks and all his travel stories. In the morning we pack our bags, the Wolf Pack gathers them and takes them to the trailer. We are required to pull the plug on the air mattress so it can be folded and stored until the next night. This is being pampered, all we have to do is pedal a mere 3,000 miles.

Today is Sunday, and Beth conducts our Sunday morning devotional service. She comes well prepared with a great scripture reading. She focuses on aspects of the journey that are difficult to do, to encourage us on this difficult adventure. If you can do this, you can assert yourself in so many other ways. The attendance is growing each week.

Today's ride has an elevation gain of more than 2,612 feet and a descent of 4,012 feet on our 82 mile ride. The past two and a half weeks we have seen very few trees, if any. We are starting to see a change in the geography and landscape. There are lots of big rolling hills in the morning and no wind which makes a big difference. Bubba mentions a slight detour today for our SAG lunch stop in Langtry, Texas. Our SAG crew set up a lunch for us at Judge Roy Bean's Museum. He was an eccentric self-proclaimed judge in Val Verde County, in Southwest Texas. Western books and films cast him as a hanging judge and he was "The Law" West of the Pecos River. The museum and his courtroom are very interesting. At one time this truly was the Wild Wild West.

Lunch is over, the wind is kicking up and we have a headwind straight in our face about 6 mph. This isn't too bad because we don't have much further to go, only about 20 miles. After leaving Langtry we reach a scenic overlook, where Mark is the only SAG team member at this stop. The view from the overlook is amazing. You can see the large canyon that the Pecos River formed, and beyond that you can see Mexico. We cross over the aqua blue water on the high level bridge about 150 ft. above the Pecos River. It is a little nerve-racking because of the narrow berm and low guard rail. Once we cross the bridge, we only have about 10 more miles to get to Seminole Canyon State Park which is our destination for the night. There is nothing around, it is very desolate.

Upon arriving at the State Park our campsite is 1-1/2 miles away from the Main Gate. The campground is set on a huge plateau with lots of low brush and no trees. Our tents are spread out over 1/4 mile radius from our eating area.

Unfortunately, after dinner I have my second leg cramp episode. It is a hard knot in my hamstring and will not go away, so I excuse myself and take a walk to loosen up. Several Wolf Pack members and riders asked if I am okay because I walk away so abruptly. When I return, they inquire about what happened and I tell them a leg cramp. It is nice to hear their concern.

During the riders meeting we are informed the DSL baskets will be outside the shower area at 6:30 am. Tonight we have NO cell phone reception and the wind picks up and the temperatures start to plummet. We are on the top of the plateau with nothing to break the wind. Better get the earplugs out if I want to get some sleep tonight and pile on another sleeping bag.

The Pecos River

Judge Roy Bean's Courtroom

THE TIME OF MY LIFE

JOURNAL DAY 24

Monday, March 25, 2019

Comstock, Texas to Brackettville, Texas

73 miles

This is our collection morning for the DSL (dirty, stinking laundry). Once again, as Bubba says, "This is huge." It is one of the big bonuses of his tour!

As a group of us head out of Seminole Canyon State Park, Zach mentions to me that we should go to the visitor center and check out the view of the canyon! Zach has ridden before so I figure he knows what he is talking about. I follow his lead. Wow what a nice view! You can see hundreds of feet of vertical rock walls.

After an hour, we pedal through a border patrol checkpoint. It looks very similar to a weigh station and for some strange reason one officer pulls me aside to ask what we are doing in the middle of Texas on bicycles. (It must be that INFORMATION sign on my forehead- whenever I travel people ask me questions!) I explained to him that there are 43 of us pedaling across the United States and he is astounded, he never thought of doing that. A couple other officers come over and wish us all luck on our travels.

At mile marker 27 we have a full SAG stop where Bubba provides all drinks, wraps and snacks. This is the place where we will be escorted over the Amistad Reservoir Bridge, a long bridge with two narrow lanes and not much of a berm to ride on. For safety reasons Bubba is our escort for almost two miles. To our right about 2-1/4 miles in the middle of the reservoir is the Mexico border. Riding along another 12 miles is the town of Del Rio. Laughlin Air Force Base is located there and it is the biggest pilot training base in the United States Air Force. John, one of our riders, trained here.

A scene from the movie *No Country for Old Men* (2007) was filmed in the Del Rio area. Two of the cast members included Tommy Lee Jones and Josh Brolin. Brackettville is famous for shooting Western movies from 1960-1994.

While we are in Del Rio for lunch we're going to Rudy's Barbecue. I choose a pulled pork sandwich which is excellent. Thanks to Adrian who recommended it. Leaving Rudy's, we head east on US-90 and are introduced to the famous chip and seal Texas road surface. Pedaling on this reminds me of a washboard, I have to keep my mouth ajar so I don't chip my teeth. Along this route we pass hundreds of working oil wells pumping 24/7. After mile marker 40, the elevation starts to level out.

As we head east each day we start to see many more trees. Today is another long day in the saddle, yet another great ride. Our destination tonight is Fort Clark Springs Camping World, 80 Scales Rd. Brackettville Texas. This is located in Ft. Clark. Buffalo Soldiers were trained and stationed here. These African - American soldiers fought in the Indian Wars battling the Apache, Comanche, and Sioux Warriors after the Civil War in 1865.

Once I have my shower, I walk around the park and talk with a man who is a welding inspector for the oil field pipeline. He lives in a modern 5th wheel travel trailer and appears to have all the comforts of home. His job is to inspect the welds on new pipelines being built to make sure they are all strong and working. He explains his job and how long he will stay in one area. He also states how he will move from campground to campground to keep up with the progress of the pipeline. His family will be staying with him for the summer when school is out in June.

THE TIME OF MY LIFE

Today's elevation gain +1,726 and loss -1,990.

Texas Bluebonnets

Journal Day 25

Tuesday, March 26, 2019

Brackettville, Texas to Concan, Texas

82 miles

Last night's stay at Fort Clark Springs was just a nice night as far as temperature goes. The Fort is located about 21 miles from Mexico and was built in 1857. The special focus was on the Buffalo Soldiers. The Fort later became the headquarters for the 2nd Cavalry Division and the 1st US Infantry Regiment, and is currently on the National Registry of Historical places, as of December 6 ,1979. The Fort was also a strong hold during the Indian Wars.

Oil Well

Heading east on Rt 90, we are on very rough Texas chip and seal roads. Today we have 2,258 feet of elevation gain. Each mile we head eastward, it is starting to look more like Ohio. Today we encounter a lot of traffic on RT 90 including long logging trucks filled with 50 ft. yellow pine logs buzzing by us in a two lane highway. YIKES!! For the most part they obey the 3 foot rule. All vehicles must remain 3 ft. from a bicyclist riding on the berm or road.

We will be in the Texas Hill Country for three full days. Some of the hills are called "Rollers," meaning if you can go fast enough downhill you may be able to make it halfway up the next hill. Other hills have a mile or so of a gradual uphill grade, then the real hill starts.

At times when the wind kicks up, you have to pedal even headed downhill. Now that makes for a long day.

At a narrow bridge, we cross over and ride into traffic on the far side shoulder, where it is wider for about 1.3 miles. At mile marker 40 we arrive in the town of Uvalde, which is the honey capital of the world. Each maintained hive can produce 4 gallons of honey a year. This is also important support for the bees pollinating crops and flowers.

We have a SAG lunch check in at Ofelia's Real Mexican. Bubba suggests we try Menudo, which is a type of Mexican soup, or have breakfast. I have met my quota of burritos on this trip. So, for lunch I order a cheeseburger. When it comes out it is HUGE. It is so big I cannot eat the whole thing. I am glad I don't try to eat the entire burger, because we still have 32 miles yet to ride and I do not want to ride on a full stomach.

After lunch we turn north and the wind now comes from our right side, riding is much better. At mile marker 65 we have a SAG check in at Shamrock Gas/Store where I go inside and buy chocolate milk, a snack, and luckily, I also remember two bars of Dove soap. After this break we have 10 more miles to our next camp site and ALL 10 miles are uphill. After 45 minutes of pedaling we turn right into Yeargans Riverbend Resort in Concan, Texas.

As I look for the Pampered Zone, I hear my name called out. Snowflake is looking for me to give me a package. It is a surprise for me to receive it and opening the package with a big smile on my face, I find a 4-port charging box. I remember speaking to my son a week ago and telling him I was struggling to get all my electronics charged. Now I can charge my bike lights and phone all at the same time. Thank you so much Nic.

There are some cabins we can stay in but more than half of us choose to stay in our own tents. The tents are set up about a 1/3 mile from The Pampered Zone and on the Frio River which is crystal clear.

About another 200 yards from our tent stands the BIGGEST tree in TEXAS. It's a Bald Cypress, the circumference is 438 inches. It is 96 ft tall and the crown spreads 112 feet. Jim W. and I walk as close as we can. We are amazed at how big this tree is. Both Jim and I, in our working careers, were in the lumber business all of our lives.

If you are lucky, you might get phone reception on the bench just outside of a cabin by the road. But today I have no such luck and the family will have to wait. Tomorrow is another very welcomed rest day which I will do zero miles on my bicycle.

THE TIME OF MY LIFE

JOURNAL DAY 26

Wednesday, March 27, 2019

Concan, Texas

Rest day

We welcome this rest day like all the others, especially this one because we are in the Texas Hill Country. Our tents are set up in a very peaceful place and we awaken to the sound of the rushing Frio River. There is no reason to get up early because breakfast is not scheduled until 8:30 so I'm staying in bed a little longer.

Today's breakfast is a full menu, complete with salmon and pancakes. Before every meal at the beginning of the food line they have hand sanitizer. Like on a cruise ship, they require everyone to use it, because of handling the same utensils when serving. This is true at all SAG stops. A little side note, We ALWAYS have to remove our riding gloves when going to the food area.

After breakfast a few of us are going down to the Frio River. Frio means cold in Spanish. This river is mentioned in the hit song, "All My Ex's Live in Texas," by George Strait released in April 1987. I have captured a few pictures of the water and raised, winding, gnarly tree roots that look like a jigsaw puzzle. The picture looks great in black and white.

One could hardly call this camping since everything is done for you. Still, most of us would choose hotels as our first choice, then school gymnasiums as our second choice. Our camping spots are usually within hearing distance of an active railroad line, complete with whistles blowing all hours of the day and night. The earplugs do come in handy.

I have a small camp chair that fits in my luggage. I have it next to my bed where I put my phone, charger, headlamp, eye mask, eyeglasses and earplugs. This has really been convenient. One time the tents were positioned under a bright mercury light and an eye mask came in very handy as well.

This area, in general, looks like Ohio, as far as the trees. We are in the middle of nowhere and there's not much to do. However, it is a rest day, so we clean our chains and some of us take naps or sit around and talk.

The only hotspot for the Internet is on a bench outside the camp office, and then it is sporadic at best. Most of us just give up trying, so we gave up the internet for a day.

Before leaving home for this trip across the country, I mentioned to our parish priest Friar Chris what I was giving up for the Lenten season. I told him I was giving up driving a car for 8 weeks. He looked at me oddly and then after a few minutes he remembered about my bike trip and he said, "What? You will be pedaling a bicycle across the United States.... Ha ha." We laughed together at that one.

Okay, time for another nap. It will be five more riding days before another rest day. There isn't really anything exciting happening today, so it's a nice time to relax and organize my three pieces of luggage. One of my duffle bags is for camping nights and one is for hotel nights. We are constantly in and out of these bags daily.

THE TIME OF MY LIFE

Journal Day 27

Thursday, March 28, 2019

Concan, Texas to Kerrville, Texas

73 miles

Waking up just before daybreak, I am renewed. I had a great night's sleep and breakfast will be served soon. This morning is foggy and misty. We start out with front and rear lights on the bike for safety. The wind is in our favor today at times, but when we make a turn and head due east, it becomes a direct headwind. Just our luck… but, yes, IT'S ALL GOOD!

When the fog finally lifts, it is another day in the saddle. Just as a side note ….as far as getting saddle sores I use Aquaphor every day. I originally bought three types: Chamois Butter, Monkey Butt and Aquaphor. I find the Aquaphor worked best for me. Riding is just a joy... to be out and about enjoying what God created for us...it's amazing. Half of today's ride is on an incline and between mile markers 17-21 it is the steepest grade we will climb on the entire trip. After nearly a month of riding we are now conditioned and just power up the hill. We all stop at the top of the hill and look at each other with grins on our faces. Just beyond the crest of the hill we have a SAG stop at mile marker 35.

Today is a very special day for another reason as well. We will be reaching our halfway point at mile marker 49.2. We have pedaled 1500 miles. Papow is at the halfway point to greet us and is our photographer. He takes single and group shots of all of us in the middle of Route 39. On our left and right at the halfway point there are fence posts, on each post is a western boot turned upside down. "WE MADE IT!" I think to myself during our short break. We have pedaled our bikes halfway across the United States. What an accomplishment it is both mentally and physically. We have 5 more days of riding before our next rest day. Our rest day coming up is in Richards, Texas at the Mexican Hill Ranch.

We will spend nineteen days crossing Texas and this is day 10. We are passing many upscale homes and ranches; the view is scenic. We think perhaps the money comes from cattle ranching, oil and gas. Many of the roads have dips and valleys to go through and in each dip, there is a flood gauge. This probably represents a wash where fast moqqving rain waters coming from the surrounding hills flow through without warning. This gauge is marked as high as five feet. We ride parallel to the Guadalupe River, and I stop and take a few pictures. The water is very clean.

At mile marker 68 we stop at Hill Country Bicycle Works in case anyone needs any necessities or accessories. After the bike shop we pick up a bike trail to head to our camp spot for the night. We are staying at Kerrville-Schreiner Park which is just across the river from the South Texas Veterans Healthcare System.

Tonight's dinner is very special because of reaching our halfway point. We have steak, lobster and baked potato with all the fixings and for dessert there are Haagen-Dazs ice cream bars. It doesn't get much better than this!

You may be wondering how our air mattresses stay inflated. Each night two of the female Wolf Pack members come through the camp around 8:00 in the evening and stop at each tent. When they announce "top off" that is our clue to check our air mattress before bedtime. As a backup plan, the Wolf Pack sets up a separate tent fondly referred to as the BOUNCE HOUSE. They inflate about six more air mattresses, so if there is a problem in the middle of the night, you can get a fresh mattress without disturbing others.

Good night from Kerrville, Texas.

Celebratory Dinner - We are Officially Half Way

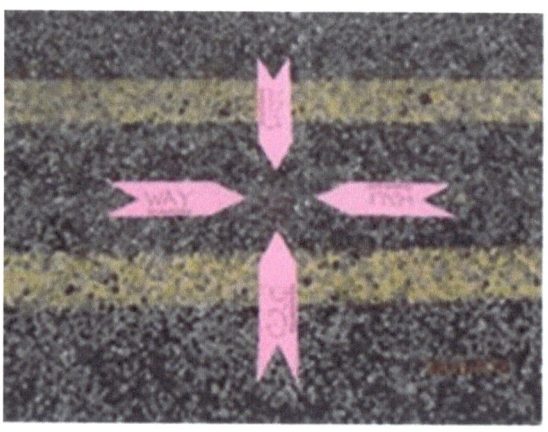

THE TIME OF MY LIFE

Journal Day 28

Friday, March 29, 2019

Kerrville, Texas to Blanco, Texas

59 miles

Today is a short riding day of 59 miles with a 2,429 ft. elevation gain There will be lots of rolling hills; we are still in Texas Hill Country. We have many left and right turns. Our route is taking us on some very quiet country roads and ranches along the way. We can see evidence of wild boar because of the way the turf is laid back. The temperature is about 70 degrees with no rain or wind.

Our first SAG stop is at the High Cafe at mile marker 17.4. This is where I have a pear muffin and a chocolate milk, this is always my go-to drink for an energy boost. Our lunch stop is at Sister Creek Winery, where Bubba provides Subway sandwiches for lunch. Many of us are puzzled because of the many vineyards in Texas, but it appears that grapes do well in the Texas Hill Country. We stop in the town of Comfort which was established in 1854 by German Immigrants who were "Free thinkers." A free thinker is a person who forms their own ideas and opinions rather than accepting those of other people, especially in religious teaching. The town's buildings are well preserved and were built with local stone. This would be an interesting town to revisit someday.

In the morning we turned in our DSL and it should be returned about 4 pm today. This laundry service is a major advantage to the trip for all of us. That's why Bubba's favorite saying is "It's all good."

We pedal along and crisscross the Blanco River numerous times. We can see that it had been a raging river a few weeks ago. At last night's riders meeting Bubba mentioned that there is a Dairy Queen 1/4 mile past where we were camping tonight. Zach and I decided to go to Dairy Queen on our own before we got to camp for the night and as a surprise to us there are about 8 other riders with the same idea.

We all hang around and talk as I eat a small mint-Oreo Blizzard. Before we get out the door, a few people ask why there are so many bicyclists? We explain what we are doing, and they are amazed at how long we have been on the road up to this date and the miles we have ridden.

Let's touch base on pedaling all day long. Months before I signed up with Bubba's Pampered Peddlers to ride such a great distance, I did much research. I looked at different kinds of bikes, tires, gearing and apparel. One decision I struggled with was to clip in or not. It's essentially a clip built into your shoe that fits into a special pedal and your foot is locked in. It takes a little practice to get used to clipping in and releasing, especially if you have to stop suddenly. I spent time asking other bikers, talking to professionals at bike shops and searching the Internet for the advantages and disadvantages. My decision was made to clip in. Through research I learned that this method gives you 14%-16% more power because you are producing power on your up pedal. Yes, one has to be prepared to unclip when the time arrives. I always unclip when approaching a stop sign or traffic light. Always remember when you clip in, you and the bike are one. Cages are a 2nd option and a 3rd option is regular pedals.

Our reservation for the night is at the Blanco State Park Campground. The park is laid out well and the restrooms and showers are very nice.

THE TIME OF MY LIFE

JOURNAL DAY 29

Saturday, March 30, 2019

Blanco, Texas to Lockhart, Texas

63 Miles

After another good night's sleep, I lie here and stretch my arms and legs to loosen up. In the morning this is my routine. During my stretch I can hear Old Glory flapping in the wind. Unzipping the tent, I am reluctant to see which way the wind is blowing. Low and behold, it is blowing from west to east, that's the way it should blow. Again, "It's all Good!"

Today's altitude gain is +1,606 ft and descent will be - 2,445 ft. This means with the wind at our backs this will be a fast day and partly sunny.

Terri, our only tandem rider, walked over a half mile from our campground to a donut shop and bought two dozen donuts to share among the riders. Many thanks Terri!

Our first SAG check in is at a school at mile marker 20, and our next one is at the Texas Pie Company in Kyle, Texas. Mmmm mouth-watering pies! Don't pass this up if you are in Kyle, Texas. After check in, we pedal 2/10 of a mile to RR Barbecue. I meet Adrian inside and he recommends the Texas beef brisket, that is what I order and it is very good. Reading from a sign in town, "Kyle Texas is the Barbecue Capital for Texas Barbecue."

Today we pass many large ranches, the front entrances and ornate gates are 150 feet long. If the entrance gate had to be built today, the cost would probably be as much as a small house in Akron, Ohio. Some of these ranches in Texas, we are told, are ten thousand acres (equivalent to 16 square miles) and the driveways could be a mile long. Wow.

We pass a large home component manufacturing plant that makes roof trusses and wall panels. For 38 years I worked for a company in Akron, Ohio. Initially I was a wall panel foreman and then moved to being a home component, engineered wood and lumber buyer.

While riding on Frontage Rd. which parallels NI-35, I hear a clicking sound on my bike. At this point I guess maybe it is a tire issue. I alert the group I am riding with that I have to stop. Upon examination of the tire I find a roofing nail in it. The nail has gone through my rear tire but misses the tube. Tom is riding with us, he is usually SAG support and a mechanic. Tom looks at it and tells me to pull it out to see if it goes flat. When Zach pulls it out with his pliers, the tire does not lose air so I keep riding. At that moment Frances, SAG support, pulls up next to me to see if all is well. I tell her yes everything is fine. I guess it pays to buy good tires. I paid good money and installed Continental Gatorskins on my bike just for this reason. Within ten minutes our head mechanic Coach pulls up next to me on the highway and asks how the tire is, and I reply, "So far, so good." Then Coach reassures me, "I will keep an eye on you and we will check it when you pull into camp." After dinner, Zach walks up to me with a smirk on his face and hands me the nail from my tire. I say, "Thanks, I think I will take this home and mount it on a plaque."

Riding through Texas, there are many different types of architecture. Some of these courthouses are spectacular, especially the Caldwell County Courthouse built in 1893. Three stories high, it is made of local stone, and has a tower with a clock face on all four sides. It is really ornate.

The scenery is changing. On these Texas roads, we pass a few oil rigs, but off the road there were hundreds, all working 24/7.

Before leaving home, my wife Mary put a St. Christopher medal on the fork of my bike to keep me safe on my journey. St. Christopher is the Patron Saint of Travelers, and so far on this trip, it has worked wonders.

Our destination tonight is Lockhart State Park. We arrive early, around 2:00 pm due to the west wind blowing at our backs all day. The tents are set up in a large circle and all I have to do is find tent #82, where a mattress is waiting for me. Not far from my tent is a golf course. After a snack and shower, I take a leisurely walk on the golf course.

Our campsite has one small pavilion so our tables and chairs are set up in a field. As evening comes and the sun goes down, so does the temperature. Today in Texas Hill Country, a good day was had by all coasters.

Journal Day 30

Sunday, March 31, 2019

Lockhart, Texas to La Grange, Texas

60 Miles

The noisy birds wake us up at the campground this morning. After 30 days of riding I now have a system down where I organize all my riding clothes together the night before and place them in the netting located at the inside top of my tent, about 6 ft off the floor. This cuts the amount of time it takes to pack my two duffle bags each morning. Then all I need to do is put my bags outside the tent and pull the plug on the air mattress. After my morning stretching routine and brushing my teeth, I walk to the Pampered Zone for coffee. Our morning conversation is usually about the weather. A few of the riders have done previous rides with Bubba and all say the weather this year has been challenging, to say the least. Other years the west to east winds were more helpful.

This morning Bubba has us make our lunch sandwiches because there will be no towns of any size that we will pass through during lunch hours. Because it is a Sunday morning, at 6:45 am Beth leads our devotional service today. More and more people have started showing up as the tour progresses showing a belief in God.

Other than that, this day is just like other days, and we all leave at staggered times and usually catch up with each other at SAG stops. Bubba and the SAG support team know where all 43 riders are or have a good idea of our location.

Today's starting temperature is 42 degrees and will top off at 55 degrees with clouds but no rain. We have lots of crosswinds, big hills and very few short, flat spots. I guess that's why they call this the Texas Hill Country.

THE TIME OF MY LIFE

We only have 60 miles to ride today, and Zach and I arrive at the Randolph Recreation Center at 1:30 pm. After showering I meet up with Zach and we decide to walk into the town of La Grange which is ten blocks away. I purchase some reading material and sunscreen. Arriving back at the Randolph Recreation Center we are just in time for snacks.

Captain Bill McArthur

After dinner, we have a guest speaker by the name of Captain Bill McArthur who is a retired astronaut. In his working years he made several trips on the International Space Station (ISS). His talk is very interesting with time for questions after. I ask him how it was to sleep in space. He answers, "It was something to get used to, I was tethered into a bag while traveling at 16,000 miles per hour in orbit around the Earth. Every one and a half hours we circled the Earth." This is very interesting to me because I have been following the Space Station for years in my hometown in Akron, Ohio. Anyone can Google International Space Station Sightings and it will give you the time and day for your area and the direction and degrees in the sky. Usually the visibility to see it in the sky lasts one to four minutes and it's visibly bright as long as it reflects the sun, then it fades into darkness.

As interesting as the talk was, I am beat. All day long it was like riding a roller coaster ride. Today's gain was 1,824 ft in the Texas Hill Country. Goodnight from LaGrange, Texas.

Journal Day 31

Monday, April 1, 2019

LaGrange, Texas to Richards, Texas

89 miles

Bubba again suggests before we leave this morning we all make our own sandwiches for lunch. We write our name on the bag, then make the sandwich, I chose ham and cheese on wheat.

One would think, in South Texas in the first week of spring it would be warm. This particular day, I have four layers of clothing on to start the day. At one point we have sleet that pelts us in the face. An arctic cold front dipped all the way to South Texas. Brrrrr.

The entire day is in the Texas Hill Country and for many miles it looks like a roller coaster. We have +3,090 ft elevation gain and -3,061 ft of descent. Our first SAG stop is at mile 22. Bubba's friend Gene is waiting for us with donuts and HOT coffee for everyone. Gene is the coffee guy. Many thanks!! Bubba has known Gene since 2010.

Our SAG lunch stop is in the town of Independence at mile 49, it's a really cold day and we are outside eating our lunch. Lunch is on the grounds of the original site of Baylor College. We can see a brick structure of 4 smokestacks left standing. Baylor is a private Baptist University in Waco, Texas and was chartered in 1845. In 2016 the tuition was $42,006 per year and the enrollment was 17,217.

THE TIME OF MY LIFE

Frank Hammer

After lunch and 20 miles later, we come to the town of Navasota. Last night at the riders meeting, Bubba mentioned he would route us past City Hall where the statue of Frank Hammer stands. For any history buff out there, Frank Hammer was the Texas Ranger who succeeded in hunting down and stopping Bonnie and Clyde. Bonnie Elizabeth Parker and Clyde Chestnut Barrow were known for armed robbery and murder. They were difficult to catch because they were always on the run from the law. They were Public Enemy #1 from 1931- 1934. They were killed on May 23,1934 in Bienville Parish, Louisiana.

We stop for a SAG check in at mile marker 69 at Dairy Queen on Wood St. The DQ is like a magnet to us bikers, we just automatically steer that way for a sweet treat. This 89 mile day is going along pretty smooth considering all the hills. To make the time go by faster I sing my theme song "America The Beautiful" rather loudly. But don't worry, no one is even remotely close enough to hear me. I still can't fathom the part about sea to shining sea. I am pedaling a bicycle this distance. Stop and think for a moment here. We all are at an average age of 65 years old, fulfilling a lifelong dream of seeing this vast country one mile at a time. Phenomenal.

Climbing back into the saddle after a bathroom break and pedaling another four miles we stop at a ranch that Is owned by a famous person by the name of Chuck Norris. (Texas Ranger) One brave coaster out of the three of us goes up to the electronic gate and hits the buzzer hoping

Chuck Norris's Ranch

Mr. Norris will come out and greet us. After a few minutes of no response, we take our pictures to remember this day and hop back in the saddle and ride away.

We have 17 more miles to ride to reach our camping destination at the Mexican Hill Ranch in Richards, Texas. It is a small cattle ranch owned by Ernie and Doris Bazan. Doris is from Germany/American and Ernie is of Mexican/ American descent. They opened the campground for Bubba and the pampered pedalers only, for the next two nights. The tents are set up in rows. Tent #82 is positioned on the outside perimeter and from my viewpoint I can take in the sights and sounds of a real Texas cattle ranch. One moooo.. right after another 24/7.

There are a few riders already in when Zach and I arrive in camp around 3:30 pm. We are just in time for the snacks and a shower. At 5:50 the rest of the riders start pedaling up the lane after a 10+ hour day in the saddle. The early riders form lines on both sides of the lane and we all start clapping and cheering them in for their accomplishment for this long day.

Did I happen to mention that in the beginning of this tour we were all strangers? After about 2 weeks into the ride, we were beginning to be closer as a group and now many of us are sharing the compassion and struggles as one unit and helping each other out during our seven and a half week adventure.

Journal Day 32

Tuesday, April 2, 2019

Richards, Texas

Rest Day

Today is our fifth rest day out of seven for the entire trip. This rest day is welcomed by all 43 riders and staff members. All of us seem to have one rule on rest days, there will be no bike riding. LOL. Today is a welcome relief from the Texas Hill Country that seemed like it would never end. We are told there will still be hills for a day and a half, but nothing like we have encountered recently.

Last night was a rather cold night sleeping in our tents. In order to get warm enough to be comfortable, I slept in my thick sleeping bag, put my thin one on top of that, then layered with my bed sheet on top of that. I also pulled in my cell phone to keep it warm. When I checked my cell phone, it was 34 degrees.

I very rarely get up in the night to go to the restroom, but last tonight it was necessary. The 100 yard walk to the restroom was very dark and very cold. As soon as I got back to my tent and climbed into my sleeping bag, everything was once again comfortable and I was able to go right back to sleep.

Morning comes fast. We all know breakfast is going to be held until 9:00 am because of the cold morning temperatures, so all of us stay a bit longer in our home away from home.

The Hay Ride

Ernie gives us a tour of his ranch and offers a hayride to anyone interested. During the hayride he stops the tractor and explains the different animals around his ranch. He has wild boar, deer, donkeys, bobcats, geese, chickens and while this is hard to believe, he even has an alligator in the pond. The ranch is small by Texas standards - only a little over 200 acres, but it is home for him and his wife Doris. Doris helps Ernie on the ranch and also sells eggs.

I have a conversation with another rider named Rose about her rides all over the United States. This is her second Coast to Coast trip with Bubba, and she has done many one week trips. As we are talking she mentions a proven way to clean your water bottles thoroughly. Rose walks to her tent and comes back with 2 Efferdent tablets. She tells me, "Put two tablets in the bottle with water, shake it around, leave it set for about 5 minutes and it will be clean." For the younger person reading this - Efferdent is for cleaning dentures. I tried this and Rose was 100% correct. Thanks a million Rose for your expert advice.

Riding through Texas in spring time there are acres of Texas wildflowers. There are blue ones called Bluebonnets and Indian Paint Brushes which are pink, and these flowers cover acres and acres. What a beautiful sight this is from just a month ago.

North of us about an hour and a half is the town of Ben Wheeler. My brother-in-law Dave visits his brother-in-law Rich, where he has a big Texas Ranch. Rich was a commercial airline pilot and likes the wide open spaces. Dave at one time was a flight instructor who owned a Cherokee single engine, with many flying hours logged flying in the cockpit. Dave was the flight instructor who taught Mary's sister Maggie how to fly his airplane.

Tonight, Ernie makes a side dish for us. It is a venison wrap with bacon and jalapeños. Ernie calls them Venison Poppers. Anne, our culinary chef makes turkey tacos with all the fixings, and chocolate cake with icing for dessert.

We have our daily riders meeting, then the temperature drops like a rock as the sun sets in the west. All the cowboys and cowgirls are headed to their tents. Today was a wonderful rest day in East Texas.

** Just a side note we have pedaled 1,735 miles and have 1,265 to go and 3 weeks remaining. **

Journal Day 33

Wednesday, April 3, 2019

Richards, Texas to Shepherd, Texas

62 miles

As dawn breaks it is 6:00 am before I get out of bed. I do my routine stretching, and then I smell the aroma of fresh brewed coffee and that is enough to finally get me moving. I dress and walk out the door, grab a cup of hot coffee and enter a discussion with four other coasters about how the weather is getting warmer and everyone is looking forward to more warmth and springtime. One would think with all the bad weather days we have had so far you might hear complaining, but to tell the truth there isn't any complaining. We all take the weather in stride. This helps with the positive attitude that is carried on throughout the trip.

Our first SAG stop is at mile marker 23.6, at Honey's Coffee and Biscuits in New Waverly, Texas just 52 miles north of the center of Houston. This is the home of famous Olympic gymnastics trainer Bela Karolyi. At Honey's, Bubba recommends an orange biscuit and coffee. It is sad to say when we arrive they are already sold out so I settle for a peach muffin. Riding on a little farther we enter Sam Houston National Forest which is in three Texas counties. For any of you hikers that may be ready, the Lonestar hiking trail is 128 miles long. The park also has camping, hunting, fishing and boating.

We pass many cattle ranches today and one particular ranch has a 12 foot high fiberglass statue of a huge steer with a sign that reads WestMont Ranch. Today once again we have many left and right turns and thankfully we have Bubba's hot pink biodegradable road arrows down on the pavement to follow. At times we feel like Hansel and Gretel following the signs to our destination. A few days ago, one of our coasters made a wrong turn and he ended up with a 100 mile plus day. This could have happened to any of us at any time.

THE TIME OF MY LIFE

Tonight's lodging is at Shepherd Sanctuary in Shepherd, Texas. This is an unusual tent cabin campground with a lot of different ornaments that are very unique. In the center of the campground there is a four foot pile of colored and clear glass wine bottles just heaped on top of each other. There is also an eight foot high playhouse for kids that they call the Grimm Abode for Grimm's fairy tales.

The Wolfpack and the married riders are in the cabins and the rest of us are staying in our tents. My #82 tent is about 45 feet from the showers and the restroom. The showers do not appear to be like the Ritz Carlton but the water is hot. So once again, "IT'S ALL GOOD." In the opposite direction of the showers is another small cabin for kids. The weather is looking a little stormy tonight, so I park my bike on the front porch of the cabin, and it's a good thing I do. Once we are in our tents for the night the clouds let loose and it rains for hours. If we had no shelter to put our bikes under on a night like this, I would secure a plastic bag over my seat to keep my seat dry. I don't want to start my day with a cold, soggy bottom.

The Shower House

JOURNAL DAY 34

Thursday, April 4, 2019

Shepherd, Texas To Silsbee, Texas

61 miles

Today a severe weather front is moving in from the Gulf of Mexico. Bubba changes our routing for the last quarter of the day. I will explain more about this later.

Most of us put our rain gear on to begin the day because it is going to be a rainy day - 100% chance. A little over an hour after we begin to ride, we reach mile marker 18.9 at the Chevron Gas Station and donut shop for our first SAG stop. This is where a chocolate milk and a donut are consumed and I leave no evidence behind...not even a crumb.

We are now in east Texas which is the beginning of logging country. Riding along the road, 40-50 logging trucks can pass us at any time. Either full of yellow pine logs headed to paper and saw mills or empty, they pass frequently. Most of the trucks give us enough room, but some blow their horn to move over to the right. Most of the time the berm is only a foot wide so there is nowhere to go. Sometimes you just hold your breath. The majority of drivers are courteous. As these trucks pass us at high speeds, sometimes there are bark chunks and pieces of wood flying at us. Most everyone wears eye protection of some kind. One of the other coasters, Jim, lives in Wisconsin and is an owner/operator of a custom saw mill. I spoke with Jim several times about lumbering operations. It was great to share our knowledge of wood working together. Jim is one of our two recumbent riders.

Our second SAG stop is at mile marker 41 at Honey Island. Today is a great day for riding because the roads are long and straight, and we only have 745 ft. of elevation gain. Even though it started out rainy, it's a nice spring-like weather day to be riding. The desert is long behind us and the greenery surrounding us is a welcome sight.

Getting back to the change in our accommodations for the night - due to the excessive rain, Bubba decided we would trade in our tents for a former school building with a dry gymnasium. Thank you to our SAG team for locating a dry night for all of us. We are staying in a YYAFA Learning Center on the corners of Route 418 and Main Street on the north side of Silsbee. A group of high school students from Indiana is staying one week on the other side of the building. These students are here to volunteer to help clean up the aftermath of Hurricane Michael last October 2018. Texas was hit hard even though this area is located miles outside of the eye of the hurricane. It has sustained much damage and the region has a long way to go to get back to normal. These high school students gave up their spring break to come to Texas. Volunteering is a powerful tool in helping with Humanity. After dinner Bubba introduced all of them and asked them why they came and they said because they wanted to help. After the talk, Zach and I walk over to a shopping plaza to look around and I buy a magazine and a local newspaper.

The showers tonight are on the cool side, but there are no complaints from anyone. This positive attitude in the group really makes it more enjoyable spending time together. Along our route today we passed many acres of blueberries in perfectly manicured rows. My wife Mary would have stopped here for a couple hours, however Bubba reminded us, "Don't touch the blueberries."

Journal Day 35

Friday, April 5, 2019

Silsbee, Texas to De Ridder, Louisiana

73 miles

Today is our nineteenth day and our last day in Texas. Texas is 1,100 miles wide from the start in El Paso to now. Today's elevation gain will be 864 ft and at this time in the trip that is virtually flat.

Our first SAG stop is at mile marker 14 at the Donut Palace where Bubba suggests ordering an orange biscuit with a chocolate milk. I always choose chocolate milk because it has protein and carbs to help during and after the ride, and it tastes good anytime.

Today is another great weather day to ride and everything around us is green. At mile marker 29 we have a SAG check in at the Valero Gas Station. Nineteen miles later we have a SAG lunch stop at a Cafe in Bon Wier, Texas. After ordering a fish sandwich, we wait patiently and talk about the ride today until one of us finally asks the waitress if she has turned in the order. She checks on it and realizes she never turned it in. She comes back and apologizes. We all think maybe she is a new hire. We agree that it's a part of life and we all have to start somewhere.

At mile marker 49 we cross over the Sabine River and enter our fifth state, Louisiana. There are a few coasters on the bridge taking pictures of the state signs, entering and leaving each state. After taking my pictures, I turn westward toward Texas and give a military salute to say goodbye to 19 days riding across Texas. What a wild ride it's been.

Rain showers are spotty today, the sun never really comes out and the temperatures are in the low 70s. Lots of logging trucks go by today, both full and empty. Most keep their distance, but there are always a few that want to prove a point and drive too close for comfort. The law is a distance of 3 feet.

Our destination tonight is the Quality Inn on 1st Street in De Ridder, Louisiana. Today's ride is leisurely and we just take it all in. Even without rushing, Zach and I arrive at 2:30 pm.

My lodging accommodation is on the first floor, and after a shower, I meander out to the Pampered Zone where I meet up with John. There are four long tables set up with white paper covering all of them. We are not sure what is going on because they have never had this set-up before. As we watch them set up, Bubba drives up and pulls out 2 big boxes and walks over to the tables. He opens the boxes and leaves them open so we can help ourselves. We look in to find fresh boiled, seasoned crawfish. To a person from Akron, Ohio this really piques my curiosity, because I have never experienced a delicacy like this before. I look over at John and ask, "What do we do next?" John says, "Watch me. You pick it up and open the shell like this. Then you get the meat out of the tail." After he puts a white towel around his neck to wipe his hands and face. John demonstrates by diving in with both hands. Crawdads are like mini lobsters and trying to get to the meat is similar. Bubba provides a spicy dipping sauce. I think they are pretty tasty but a lot of work. They are certainly a Cajun delicacy. (A little more on this later)

Crawfish Snack

Bubba gives Anne and Serge the night off and will be treating us to dinner at Presley's. The only catch is we have to walk about a third of a mile. After dinner, while walking back to the hotel, I decide to treat Mike, John and Zach to Dairy Queen to top off the evening.

Arriving back at the hotel, I call Mary as I usually do when phone reception is available. I also call my friend Lynn. He and I have been friends for over 60 years in Akron, Ohio on Miller Avenue.

Here is a random trivia question - "Good Night Mrs. Calabash wherever you are." This is a famous saying at the end of a television show from the 50s and 60s. Can you guess what show? The answer will be at the end of tomorrow's entry.

THE TIME OF MY LIFE

JOURNAL DAY 36

Saturday, April 6, 2019

DeRidder, Louisiana to Opelousas, Louisiana

91 miles

I have a great night's sleep at the Quality Inn; it's a big change from a couple nights ago, hearing wind and rain on the tent all night long. I walk down to the hotel lobby for breakfast. At all hotel stays we are required to take our bags out to the baggage trailer area so they can be loaded by the Wolf Pack. When we start out this morning we need our front and back lights on because of the fog. We can feel the heaviness of the humidity in the air.

Today is going to be a warmer day, there is no rain in the forecast and we have a little over 800 ft of elevation gain. The only catch is the 91 miles, but by now with everything I have done, it is really no big deal. It's just another day in the saddle heading home.

Our first SAG stop is at mile marker 20. Yep, you guessed it… behind the SAG stop is a donut shop, and yes, they have chocolate milk, even in Oberlin, Louisiana. We have many turns on this route today but so far, it's been a good day. If you think about it, all we have to do is pedal.

Today we are pedaling past many crawfish ponds. We take time out to watch them being harvested. Crawfish are harvested around Easter, in the spring. Baited pyramid traps are set in the flooded fields. These fields are rotated each year, one year rice, next year crawfish. They use a small flat bottom boat to go through the fields, pick up the baskets and dump them into a basket on the boat. These flooded fields are shallow, maybe 14 -20 inches deep.

At mile marker 64 we come upon the town of Mamou. Bubba said the whole trip is planned around this town, so we can have a cultural experience at Fred's Lounge. At 420 6th Street every Saturday afternoon there is a live broadcast with a band playing Zydeco music. This is a mix of rhythm and blues and Louisiana creole. The establishment isn't very big and it is crowded and the music is very loud. Zach and I go in and listen to one song. Then we decide to walk across the street to the Crazy Cajun Cafe. Inside the cafe we find Bubba along with 15 coasters ordering lunch. Bubba asks me what I think about the music. I reply, "You just don't hear that kind of music in Akron, Ohio."

The last third of the day, the headwinds pop up again with only about 30 miles to go. These winds are not as bad as Arizona and Texas. Zach and I always take notice which way the flags are blowing. We point out anything that is blowing in the wind, and we make a game out of it. We just keep laughing and shaking our heads. Plus, it is something to distract us.

Tonight's stay is in Opelousas, which is the oldest town in Louisiana. We are at the Holiday Inn. To be perfectly honest all these days and nights are starting to run together with this jaunt across the country. I am living out my childhood dream which is no longer a dream, and I am having the time of my life. While growing up I used to lie in bed at night and look at maps of the States and read through sets of encyclopedias to learn and dream about traveling. This pedaling adventure sure wins the prize compared to lying in bed reading about it.

The answer to yesterday's trivia question about Mrs. Calabash ...... this is what Jimmy Durante said at the end of his tv show.

THE TIME OF MY LIFE

Journal Day 37

Sunday, April 7, 2019

Opelousas, Louisiana to St. Francisville, Louisiana

68 miles

Today is Sunday and it seems like everyone is up early. We gather in the meeting room for coffee. Our topic of discussion this morning is how everyone has a positive attitude toward our daily rides regardless of what our conditions are. I look forward to Sundays, we will have our weekly non-denominational service led by Beth in the hotel meeting room. She's a good speaker and seems to find the right words for this trip.

There was a mix up in communication between Anne and Bubba. Anne thought because we were at a hotel we would be eating breakfast at the hotel facility. Because of the mix up Bubba makes an announcement, he will buy breakfast at the Waffle House, 1/2 mile from the hotel. By the time Zach and I get to the Waffle House the line is out the door, so the two of us turn around and head to the McDonalds, 6 miles on US 190 E.

We start out with our daily route sheets, showing many left and right turns with slight rolling hills. Finally, we reach old US Rt 90, which is closed to traffic. Bubba has permission for us to ride on this old desolate road. Bubba warned us about the conditions of the road. There will be potholes and the fact that it is level with the swamp means we may encounter an alligator or snakes. The road stretches out for five and a half miles in front of us and it is an experience to see the bayou country and the Mississippi River Delta region. We pedal slowly to watch for hazards and we fortunately do not encounter any wildlife or reptiles on the road. We reach the end of the road and off in the distance we can see Coach, our tour mechanic, sitting in his van. He's waiting to see if anyone has a mechanical issue; I always give him a thumbs up.

We make a stop at the Pointe Coupee Parish Museum, it is closed. We forgot it is Sunday. We stop for lunch at New Roads, Louisiana at mile marker 44. Behind the Subway store is the False River which was once a part of the Mississippi River. Today, it is a long u-shaped lake. It was cut off from the main Mississippi in 1722 by seasonal flooding and the power of the water cut a shorter channel to the east.

The John Audubon Bridge

After lunch we pass many homes with well-manicured lawns and on the opposite side of LA-10 E we can see the huge dike that holds back the waters of the Mississippi River. Looking into the distance we see the John Audubon Bridge that we will eventually pedal over in order to cross the wide Mississippi River. The approach to the bridge is a long grade of about 4%. Once on top of the bridge in the middle of the Mississippi River we stop to take pictures. The height of the bridge at that point, I guess to be about 200 ft above the water. As we continue to ride eastward, we all notice the land on the left and right of us for about a mile is flooded.

We have 14 miles, or less than one hour, until we reach our night's lodging.

Did I mention that my wife Mary velcroed a St. Christopher medal on my bike? St. Christopher is the Patron Saint of travelers. I also received a blessed medal from Margaret, my former wife, to keep me safe on my journey.

Our ride today took us through Atchafalaya National Heritage Area. This is the largest wetland and swamp in the United States of America. Atchafalaya derives from the Choctaw term meaning long river. From my viewpoint, I picture it as a "funnel" that takes all the water from the central and southeast United States and funnels it into the basin and eventually the Mississippi River to the Gulf of Mexico.

Some of today's roads have small berms which have rumble strips and If you hit one on your bicycle it will jar your teeth. We pretty much pedal on the road to avoid this hazard.

Today's high temperature is 86 degrees and for once it feels great to ride in the hot humid south compared to the frigid, cloudy days we rode just a month ago. This area has many cotton plantations with large southern mansions. One would have to remember back in your history books, the slaves that worked on these plantations were not paid wages, but were given minimal clothing and food, and some were housed or given resources to build their own shelter. But thanks to Abraham Lincoln and the Emancipation Act Of 1863 declared, "that all persons held as slaves shall be forever free."

Tonight's stay is at Marydale Girl Scout Camp in St. Francisville, Louisiana, which is a mile off of Marydale Road. Located in West Feliciana Parish, St. Francisville was a cotton export center in its prime. We will be here two nights and Bubba gives us the option of staying in cabins or the main building. Half of us chose the main building because of the close proximity to dining and shower areas. Tomorrow is a rest day and we have one more rest day before this adventure ends. After a hot shower I look at my watch and it is 4:00 which means snacks are put out by Anne. Today we have hummus, tortilla chips, with 4 kinds of brick cheese and fresh fruit.

The sky grows dark during dinner and a thunderstorm moves through the area. We take cover in a screened pavilion. The wind and rain blow sideways, but we manage to stay dry. So... once again, "IT'S ALL GOOD!"

After dinner there are some laundry items left in the baskets and Bubba puts on a little comedy show upon returning these items. I, for one, write down a list of everything I turn in to the DSL and when it comes back I cross it off my list. Other coasters take pictures of their items to make sure they retrieve all of them.

THE TIME OF MY LIFE

Nancy and Peter

Journal Day 38

Monday, April 8, 2019

St. Francisville, Louisiana

Rest Day

On rest days breakfast is served from 8 - 8:30. Anne prepares another great breakfast for us with eggs, bacon, sausage, toast, bagels, fruit, cheeses, oatmeal, French toast, smoked salmon and yogurt. For beverages we have an assortment of juices, coffee, teas, and milk.

At 10:00 am Bubba offers a shuttle for anyone who would like to go to St. Francisville to tour the town. There are a few who choose to go on the tour but ride their bikes into town. John and I decide to go with them in the van and he drops us off in the center of town, which used to be the former Cotton Capital of the south. Our visit to explore this historic part of town is short. First, we go to the visitor center and talk to a few locals. One of the local volunteers asks us, "what brings you to this town?" John and I look at each other and John says, "You tell her." And then I reply, "No you tell her, you have rank!" John tells her we are pedaling our bicycles across the United States. It amazed them that we are a group of mostly senior citizens taking on such a huge task. They cannot fathom riding a bicycle that far. Upon leaving they wish us well.

One would never realize near this small town in West Feliciana Parish, just 22 miles to the Northwest on the Mississippi River, is the Louisiana State Prison. This prison is nicknamed the Alcatraz of the south and is the largest maximum-security prison in the United States. It was named Angola after the African country. Angola Prison sits on 18,000 acres of the 28 square miles of a former plantation larger than the city of Manhattan, New York.

After walking another block, we come across a cedar tree that is growing inside of an oak tree. There is a sign located near the trees that reads, 'Two trees in one, created by God over 100 years ago.'

These trees are amazing to me, since I worked in the lumber field since age 18.

Today is Monday and some shops in town are closed. John and I do walk to a coffee shop, where John treats me to cheesecake and coffee. We ask a waitress to take our picture for memories. It is enjoyable to just sit, talk and relax quietly, instead of constantly moving.

At this point in the trip we are all in excellent physical cycling shape. We only have one more rest day coming up and that will be Dauphin Island, Alabama. After that, we will be looking at our last 9 days and 524 miles across Florida with no more days off.

We take the shuttle back to Marydale Girl Scout Camp. After lunch I clean my bike and oil my chain, and I try to do this every 5-6 days. I must keep this well-oiled machine in good shape because this is what will get me back to Mary. I walk back to my sleeping area and organize my personalbelongings once again, so I can find what I need in the shuffle. After I complete the task, I take a shower and meet up with Zach. It's humid here and warm, I comment to Zach, I couldn't imagine living here in the summer time.

Zach suggests we tour the cabins where the others are staying. There are also cabins on stilts and in another area, there is a riding stable, but no horses are available at this time.

After dinner and during the riders meeting Bubba briefly reviews the tail end of the trip, which is fast approaching. It is only two weeks away. We all need to know what the procedure is and what to expect. One important item to Bubba is for us, as a group, to choose someone who will lead us into the beach at St Augustine, Florida. This is our food for thought, until the next meeting. Later that evening I approach Bubba and suggest Greg from Ohio to lead us into the beach. Greg has had to overcome several significant hurdles planning for this type of adventure. Greg is a true inspiration to all of us.

Finally, it's back to my sleeping area to update my Instagram with pictures, answer emails and voicemails. By the time I finish all this it is close to 9 pm and Coach makes the announcement, "Ten more minutes 'till lights out."

THE TIME OF MY LIFE
JOURNAL DAY 39

Tuesday, April 9, 2019

St. Francisville, Louisiana to Franklinton, Louisiana

86 miles

I have another great night's sleep. We have a complete breakfast with all the fixings; not bad for a camping breakfast. After breakfast we all ride out of the Girl Scout camp like a row of ducks. We have a mile to go before reaching US-61S. On the highway for just half a mile, we enter an elementary school zone where all traffic is stopped. The children are getting dropped off for school. Not far after the school we turn due east and the sun is in our eyes.

Before I left for the trip, my wife Mary cut the bill off of a ball cap and velcroed it inside the helmet. This has been a nice gesture worth a million dollars because the added bill helped with the sun, rain, sleet, snow and even the cold winds. "Thanks Mary!"

Our first SAG stop is at mile 26 at Main Street Market. Our second one is at the Hatfield Store near mile marker 47. Our lunch stop is at mile 58 at the Cafe in Kentwood, LA.

During our ride today, Bubba has a suggestion. During Bubba's ten years of conducting coast to coast bike tours, he befriended a man named Earl. He is a pleasant elderly southern black gentleman who lives in a shack and does not have much. Bubba mentioned the night before that if anyone gives him a couple dollars it would be greatly appreciated.

Each year Earl sits on his front porch and looks forward to seeing the 40 + riders come through town. It is an exciting time for him in this small town of Clinton, La.

Tonight we are staying at Hillcrest Baptist Church located in Franklinton, La. The gym is not large enough to accommodate all of us, so Bubba inquires, by a show of hands, who would like a tent set up. Zach and I both choose our tents along with 22 others.

Arriving at our night's destination at 3:30 pm, it was a very nice relaxing day pedaling on our 86 mile route. The wind, along with a bright sunny day, sure is a blessing. "Life is Good." A couple of us riders have a game we play for entertainment. We try to find our tent number in a field of tents. I spot mine in the back row, unload my bike bag and prop my bike up against the fence. I just happen to notice not far from my tent is a cemetery but I'm not concerned. All the residents are resting, hopefully in peace.

I enjoy a hot shower, then walk over to the Pampered Zone and have some snacks. After our 6:00 dinner it is announced the rider meeting will be at 8:00 tomorrow morning. The meeting tonight is postponed due to a weather front coming in. We have a short riding day tomorrow, therefore there will be plenty of time to have the meeting.

Today is a warm and sunny day and hydration is always a number one priority. Just like many others, I do not want to succumb to leg cramps. Today I drank three 20 oz. bottles of water and one 20 oz. Gatorade. Keep in mind we are in Louisiana and our elevation gain is 2,628, yet we never went over 375 feet above sea level. There are a lot of ups and downs.

In regards to sleeping in a tent, National Guard Armory, school gymnasium or hotel, I personally have no problem with any of the accommodations, but my first preference is a hotel.

At the beginning of the trip there was a three hour time difference from the east coast where I live to the west coast where we started. When we all went to bed at 9:00, it was actually midnight and it was too hard for me to go to sleep. It took me a couple days to adjust.

THE TIME OF MY LIFE

Journal Day 40

Wednesday, April 10, 2019

Franklinton, Louisiana to Poplarville, Mississippi

45 miles

At the start of today we have the sun directly East and it is glaring in our eyes for almost an hour. Thank goodness for sunglasses. To add to that we have an elevation gain of 1428 but there are eight miles that are almost flat in the middle of our nice warm day. Bubba has learned from experience that since it's a short day we have time for the riders meeting in the morning. The 45 miles we will go today will take us about 4-5 hours, and we do not have access to our nights lodging in the National Guard Armory until 2 pm.

Our first SAG stop is at the Donut Palace at Bogalusa, which is two miles from the Mississippi border. Mississippi is the sixth state we will pedal through.

At mile marker 39 we turn on Sam Smith Rd. You can see the town of Poplarville a few miles ahead. Poplarville is the Blueberry Capital of Mississippi. Lunch is at Scooters and then a few of us drift across the street to the Pearl River Drug Store. To our amazement they have an old time soda fountain that looks very similar to the one on the Andy Griffith Show from the early sixties. For those of us who are old enough to remember, Ellie Walker was the name of the drug store pharmacist on the Andy Griffith Show. Her real name was Elinor Donahue. I decide to have a scoop of Mint Chocolate chip ice cream. Browsing around the old fashioned drug store, I spot a small bottle of Visine. Since I am running low, I decide to buy it. The owner of the drug store / clothing store comes over to talk to Zach and me. He is a southern gentleman, slow talking and very nice. He asks us how our trip is going, so we fill him in and wish him a good day.

Zach and I walk up to the courthouse, we take pictures of the rose garden in full bloom and some pictures of Civil War statues. Recently there have been articles written in the newspaper about displaying the Confederate flag in public places. There is a movement to keep it alive, but keep the display in a museum setting because it is a part of U.S. history without any controversy. The Civil War has been over for 154 years.

Along the southern tier across the United States we encounter many unleashed dogs just waiting to chase us, at least to the edge of their property. Well today is our lucky day. The first dog is a pit bull, running full speed from a hidden driveway, his objective with his white gleaming teeth, is my right foot. At last night's riders meeting we were reminded to stay on high alert for these dogs from past experience. This one particular pit bull led me just like a Tom Brady pass to one of his receivers. My mind and hand react simultaneously. I shift gears and it gives me enough speed and distance to pull away from him. I am sure the dog will just wait for the next group of riders. We were told when dogs start to chase you, yell in a loud stern voice "NO, Go Home." It will work most of the time, but not today! The second dog must have had a shock collar on because he stopped at the property line.

A short ride today of 45 miles is received well by all, it is almost a rest day. Tonight's stay will be at the Poplarville National Guard Armory, which is also the local hurricane shelter. One could only imagine going through a hurricane with very strong winds for hours without stopping. Hurricane Michael hit this area in October 2018.

Casey, Zach and I find empty rooms for the night which have our own electrical outlet. We snore some, so we try to be considerate of others by getting isolated. DSL will be collected tomorrow morning so tonight I gather my laundry and make a list of what I will turn in.

After dinner several of us walk over to an indoor riding arena and watch cattle roping. Walking back to our dinner area Anne has set out ice cream sundaes for dessert. It can't get any better than this. Lights out is at 9:00 pm. Casey calls me over to his corner room and we can't find the light switches to turn out the lights. I mention to Casey maybe because it's a hurricane shelter the lights stay on all the time. Casey suggests we get our eye masks ready for the night.

On August 29, 2005, Hurricane Katrina inflicted heavy damage with wind gusts up to 135 mph at Pearl River Community College. The 134th Field Artillery National Guard Unit spent 3 weeks after the destruction helping the community.

Since it's a short day I think maybe I will give you a little information on my first bicycle. When I was eight years old I won a bicycle at Summit Beach Amusement Park in Akron, Ohio. This park was four houses down the street from my house. This was my first bicycle, I had to learn to ride my Stingray bicycle with monkey handlebars and a banana seat. The odometer was the size of a hardball and the front light was the size of a softball. My older sister Marylou helped teach me how to ride. Each day I would rush home from St. Bernard's Grade School so I could ride my bike. I put a speedometer on the bike and pedaled twenty miles most days, never thinking 60 years later I would be pedaling across the United States.

Poplarville, Mississippi

Journal Day 41

Thursday, April 11, 2019

Poplarville, Mississippi to Ocean Springs, Mississippi

70 miles

Happy Birthday Mary! This will be the first birthday we've missed together in 34 years. I felt bad before I left, but Mary reassured me to go and have the trip of a lifetime. On February 25, I wrapped Mary's gifts and placed them in the lower cabinet of my workshop. I will FaceTime her after she gets home from work and guide her to the birthday presents.

Today's 70 mile ride is on a smooth road with only 1,947 ft elevation gain. Our weather is absolutely perfect, and our first SAG stop is at mile marker 24 which is the parking lot for Biloxi Creek Church. Our next stop is for lunch at Ramsey Creek Baptist Church (12 miles east of Saucier, Mississippi) where the women in the church have prepared lunch for us with an assortment of cheeses and barbecue beef, roast beef and ham. To accompany this delicious lunch was coleslaw, baked beans and dessert. We thank these women by giving them a donation for taking time out of their day to prepare the lunch and for their spiritual support.

Tonight's stay is at Ocean Springs, Mississippi at the Super 8 Hotel. Once again after a shower, we can collect our DSL. Our SAG support team does a fantastic job for us throughout the whole trip. At times they also share their experiences of their rides across the United States with Bubba. In order to be eligible to become a SAG team member, you have to have biked across the US.

Later in the afternoon, sitting in the Pampered Zone, I FaceTime Mary to wish her a Happy Birthday. When I tell her where to find her gifts, she starts laughing and says, "Ohh that box was for me?" She was cleaning the basement while I was gone and found them, but thought maybe they were for the grandkids so she didn't pay any attention to them. Mary goes down to my workshop and unwraps them while we are on the phone together, she is excited. The gift is more of a joke than a gift, for now anyway. It is 2 bags of unsalted nuts and a bag of pistachios, her favorite. She is very excited because she loves nuts, maybe that's why she loves me.

I FaceTime my son and his family, and also call our friends Gary and Diane in Alliance, Bill K. in Akron, and Joe and Melinda in Lorain, Ohio to let them know my progress.

It is so hard to believe how far we have already pedaled and the sights we have seen crossing our country. Last evening I figured that my tire on my bicycle would go around 2,160,982 revolutions on this trip. I can't wait to get home and talk to Maria, who was our spin class instructor at the Green YMCA, I want her to know that I made the entire trip and finished.

CLARENCE BECHTER

JOURNAL DAY 42

Friday, April 12, 2019

Ocean Springs, Mississippi to Dauphin Island, Alabama

78 miles

I wake up today after a good night's sleep, have breakfast in the motel dining area and we leave like a flock of birds headed eastward. Eventually we all drift apart with picture taking, restroom breaks, sightseeing, etc. On the longer days we are sometimes 30 miles apart, but most everyone is in by about 4 pm. We often think 4 pm is the magical time that Anne and Serge set up the snack area.

Our first SAG stop is at mile marker 29 at a coffee shop, I have a cup of coffee and a coffee roll. It really hit the taste buds at 10 in the morning. Yum.

We make a right turn out of the coffee shop onto MS- 613S and then a quick turn onto MS-614E, then pedaling six more miles we enter our 7th State, Alabama. Our next SAG stop is mile marker 43 at a gas station/store. We talk briefly about the realization that at this point we only have one more state to go. There is a small crowd of coasters outside the store and I pedal up to a gas pump and pretend I am filling my bike up with gas. Everyone just laughs and shakes their head, and someone says, "There he goes again."

Our SAG stop for lunch is at the Catalina Bayou Restaurant, 14060 S. Wintzell Ave. in Bayou La Batre. The restaurant is recommended by Bubba. This area is known as the fish and shrimp capital of Alabama. I have a fish dinner and three glasses of lemonade. Several movies have been filmed and featured in this area, *Pirates of the Caribbean, The Curse of The Black Pearl* and *Forrest Gump*.

After lunch we only have 20 miles to go before we have our last rest day of the trip. This is once again another perfect riding day. Thinking back, it sure beats riding in the previous headwinds, rain and snow, with logging trucks whizzing by. Pedaling on we make a right turn onto Dauphin Island Parkway and the view opens up to Mobile Bay and about 5 miles away you can see the bridge with the big bump in the middle. The first bridge was destroyed by Hurricane Frederic in 1979 and was replaced in 1982. This bridge formerly was the Gordon Parsons Bridge named after the 46th Governor of Alabama. The bridge has to be high enough to let ocean vessels pass underneath and the clearance below is 83 ft. Wow! That is an eight story building and what a bump in the road it is. Going down was fun, but you had to watch the winds coming across Mobile Bay. In previous years some of the coasters had to walk up the incline because of the extreme wind.

Once over the bridge, the winds die down. We stop to take pictures and we are amazed at the number of seagulls hovering overhead. The gulls are possibly waiting for fishing boats to return. Once on the island it is absolutely flat land, and we have not seen this since we left San Diego beach when we first started March 2, 2019.

While riding past the beach front homes we see a group of people standing close to the road, getting closer and closer we hear cow bells. The residents of the island are out here to cheer us on and welcome Bubba and his Coast 2 Coast tour, all 43 riders. A welcome like this puts a boost of energy and adrenaline in all of us.

We have another mile and a half to go before reaching our destination for the night, The Dauphin Island Campground. Our tents are set up in a mature yellow pine forest, about 200 yards from the Gulf of Mexico. Less than 60 yards away is a nice picnic shelter with sides on it. A brand new masonry shower facility stands constructed another 100 yards away.

Once I am settled into the tent, all I want to do is go down to the beach. As I pass a motorhome the owner comes out. We introduce ourselves and Carl inquires what the story is behind the group. I take a few minutes to fill him in on our adventures. After speaking with him awhile, he tells me to watch for the Copperhead snakes on the path while I walk to the beach. I thank him and I head down to the beach. The sand is white like sugar. While walking on this beach and looking out at the water, the winds are gusting on the Gulf of Mexico. The water has white caps. A few miles out I can see several oil rigs. We are told the water around the rigging location is 20 foot deep. On my way back and at camp, I tell others about the Copperhead snakes near the path to the beach.

After a hot shower I have time to write in my journal and post on Instagram. It's hard to believe we only have 9 more days to get to St. Augustine.

After finishing, I call Bill K., a fellow I met at Panera Bread on Arlington street in Akron, Ohio. He was my mentor when training for mountain climbs and training for this bike adventure. Bill has run 14 marathons including Boston, many half marathons and ran Pikes Peak, along with hiking many sections of the Appalachian Trail. Thank you, Bill, for all your support and words of encouragement.

Now we are settled into the campground and tomorrow is our last rest day of the trip. This is the part I like - the next five meals we eat we won't have to eat and run, we can sit, relax and enjoy the food and conversation.

JOURNAL DAY 43

Saturday, April 13, 2019

Dauphin Island, Alabama

Rest Day

Today is our seventh and last rest day of our trip. The next nine days we will ride all the way through Alabama and Florida. We have 541 miles to go.

It is a nice spring morning and there is absolutely no reason to get up early, except for the smell of bacon and coffee. By the time I dress and leave the tent, there are a dozen coasters already having coffee, and I meander over to join them. We enjoy another outstanding breakfast by Anne, eggs Benedict, sausage, bacon, home fries, jellies, coffee and juices. After this delicious breakfast I go for a walk on the white sugary sand not far from our encampment. Walking about 3/4 of a mile down the beach, I take pictures. One particular picture is of a wave hitting a large log. It takes me three tries to get the right shot, but now it is forever frozen in time, with the water splashing up in the air. As I look out over the water I notice many oil and gas platforms for drilling in the Gulf of Mexico. There are so many different things to see out here on my journey; I would never have seen them if I stayed in Ohio. I am so thankful for the opportunity to join, and soon to complete, this exciting adventure.

Here is an honest true fact, we have been pedaling across the United States for six weeks and I would consider myself in good shape. But as I have been writing and you have been reading, you are probably wondering about all our food consumption. The truth of the matter is, I don't believe I have lost one pound, not one.

As I walk back to camp, I see Carl from Minnesota coming out of his RV and stop to talk with him again. Carl is an official snow bird and makes Dauphin Island his winter home with his wife. I think this area is a good choice to come to in the wintertime. I enjoy our conversation.

Since today is a rest day, let's talk about leg cramps. I am always concerned about leg cramps because I get them at home, usually when I climb ladders and get up and down off the floor at a job site. I am concerned about the daily physical exertion on my legs. I am very aware of how much liquid I consume for hydrating. I eat extra bananas and drink pickle juice at every SAG stop. I even take magnesium pills, and I believe all of this has been helpful. I experienced one cramp on the first day, March 2nd, going into the foothills east of San Diego. We were in a residential neighborhood and no one was around. I jumped off the bike and walked it off. Then I got back on to keep pedaling. That evening, I had a long talk with God about this. I let him know I had 3,000 miles to go and I needed a little help. I only had one other episode and that was at Seminole Canyon State Park on March 23rd.

A little after breakfast Zach wants to know if I am interested enough to go to the camp store and to Fort Gaines. This Fort is within walking distance of our camp. This was a Civil War Fort that protected Mobile Bay from ships coming in to a port. This is where Admiral Farragut spoke the famous words "Damn the Torpedoes, full speed ahead."

THE TIME OF MY LIFE

We take a self-guided tour and discover the sleeping quarters, the mess hall and the latrine. The latrine is very interesting. The waste exited out of the Fort in a chute and it headed toward a ditch and when the tide came in, it took the waste out. Not too far from the latrine is a thick brick wall and you can see an indentation from a cannon ball that was fired at the Fort. On top of the Fort, it is very windy coming off the Gulf of Mexico. Zach and I just look at each other and at the same time say out loud, "I hope these winds die down before we leave in the morning!" Then we laugh.

It is close to 12:30 and our lunch time, so Zach and I head back to camp where Anne is setting up the serving line. She has a picnic lunch consisting of hot dogs, cheese burgers, potato and macaroni salad, mixed fruit and some vegan options. After eating and conversing a bit we all agree it is time for a well-deserved afternoon nap.

Approximately 40 minutes later, I wake up and unzip the tent to spot one of the Wolf Pack members, Jordan, giving haircuts. When I inquire about the wait she says, "close to an hour." So, I get in line. She is going to school for cosmetology and is offering haircuts for practice. She does a great job, and we all tip her.

After my haircut, I walk over and enter the pavilion where 3 coasters are putting together a 1500 piece jigsaw puzzle. They mention that hopefully they will have it completed by the end of the day.

Before we started this trip in San Diego, Bubba asked us not to discuss three things, politics, religion and sex. There are still numerous topics to discuss with this group who started out as strangers 6 weeks ago.

I notice Alyssa is cleaning bikes on a rack with Coach's instructions. I walk over and ask her if she will detail my bike and oil my chain. She comments, "There is one bike ahead of you, so the wait won't be long." I park my bike next to a tree and come back later to pick it up. She does a great job and I give her a good tip for the time she spent on it. Great Job Alyssa! Thank you!

The balance of the day I spend going for another walk on the beach and a short jaunt over to the ferry dock where we will depart tomorrow morning. This ferry will transport us across Mobile Bay to Fort Morgan. The ferry does not run when the waters are choppy and hopefully in the morning the winds will slow down.

Since this is a rest day I would like to inject some notes that I have written over the past several weeks. While listening to other riders some had names for their bikes from the start. It didn't take me very long to name my Jamis bike. From this day forward, it was christened Shorty-Retta. Some of you may have guessed it already, I named it after my mom and dad. So, in a sense they rode with me across America.

We all have a lot of respect for Bubba, a retired detective from St Louis, Missouri. In a sense he is like a duck, paddling like crazy underneath the water but calm on the surface. He always adds humor in his meetings. He also thinks of a lot of things ahead of time that you might not. For instance, the tour recommended getting a tetanus shot before the trip, in case of a mishap. This information comes from knowledge and experience.

Every riding day before starting out we have the anticipation of seeing new sights and sounds around each curve in the road and up and over the mountains. On our shorter riding days arriving earlier in the afternoon, we sit around and discuss different topics like occupations we had such as lawyers, retired military, lumber mill owners, teachers, ship workers, judges, professors, office equipment repairman, software engineers, lumber buyer. We have a very diverse group together for this ride.

On one rest day Daniel and I sat and talked and he shared what he does for a living while traveling all over the world as a contractor with the military. Another discussion was geocaching with Hance and Ann. I learned something new and I had no idea about it before our discussion; it seems like an interesting hobby.

THE TIME OF MY LIFE

Dave (Coach) is our tour mechanic, a very likable person with lots of interesting stories. At the end of one particularly long day he set up fixing a few flat tires and cleaned out his van. As we watched, he pitched about a dozen or so used inner tubes out of the van onto the ground. We were amazed at all the flats we had this day and how quickly he was able to change them.

Late afternoons and evenings are the best time to call or FaceTime home. On a couple occasions Greg would be hanging around while I was talking and he would always say, "Hello Mary," so I would hand him the phone so he could get to know her until they actually meet in Florida.

While riding down the road we see flowers and memorials set up on the side of the road, for a loved one who may have passed away in an automobile accident at that particular spot. There were a lot more of these than anyone could imagine.

I am amazed that there are a few of the 2019 coasters who have toured with Bubba on previous trips. Daniel is on his fourth trip. Rose, John, Jane, Zach, Adrian, Henry, and Mike are all repeat riders. Whew... I think once is enough for me, but you never know.

Journal Day 44

Sunday, April 14, 2019

Dauphin Island, Alabama to Pensacola, Florida

55 miles

Palm Sunday

Last night we all went to sleep under a canopy of tall yellow pine trees. At 3 am we are all tucked in Bubba's Kelty dome tents and I think I am having a dream. I wake up to a loud shrill noise and I see a flashing light in my tent. At first, I think someone is calling me on the phone, but when I look at it, I see a TORNADO warning. I immediately get up, throw my valuables in a bag and place my personal belongings on top of my air mattress. I rush 100 yards to our shower/restroom facility which is a new masonry structure. Along the way I hear the thunder and see lightning and the rain is pouring down. These tall pine trees are bending with the winds. The way the wind is blowing any of these trees could land on our tents and cause a tragic situation. To my surprise there are 25 or so other campers in the building along with C2C riders. We wait the storm out for about 45 minutes. I check my NOAA weather map app. The good news is that it is a fast moving front and the tail end is just over us now.

When it's completely gone, I walk back to my tent and unzip the door to find water in my tent. The tent happened to sit in a low spot and the water came in. Lucky for me I put my bags on the air mattress so they were dry. I walk back to the dining hall and find a spot to lay down for the balance of the night. There are about a dozen other coasters that join me. Before going back to sleep, I lay there and think of all the folks that stayed in their tents and what could have happened. In my opinion, it's better to be safe than sorry.

Last night was like a dream with the tornado siren going off. We learned that a tornado did touch down within a few miles of us. Scary. It's hard to believe it is Palm Sunday already. Beth gathers us together before breakfast for our devotional service. It is surprising to see more and more coasters attending as the weeks go on.

Ernie from California will leave the tour this morning because of a family emergency. I wish him well as we say our goodbyes. While that is disappointing news, all is well this morning with clear blue skies and sunshine. We talk among ourselves about the water being too rough to take the ferry across Mobile Bay. We are glad to see the sunshine. We are all to meet at the Ferry dock at 8:00 am. The Captain of the ferry informed us he has the all clear and it's okay to cross the Bay.

We can't find Bubba anywhere around this morning and wonder where he is. Someone spots him at the helm of the ferry and shortly after, he gets on the PA system. What a hoot this is. The ferry ride is 4 miles across Mobile Bay, passing a few gas and oil rigs on the way. Bubba had told us the night before that these were the ONLY four miles we did not have to pedal to get to St Augustine, but if you wanted to make up these four miles you were welcome to do it. LOL While on the ferry the seven Coasters from Ohio, have a group picture taken. Ohio is the most represented state on this year's tour with Gregg, Nancy, Peter, Mike, John, Toph and me. Disembarking from the ferry, we ride along a smooth road with a tailwind pushing us and Mobile Bay on our left and the Gulf of Mexico on our right for about 17 miles. The traffic today is almost non-existent.

At mile marker 32 THERE IT IS, the sign that reads "WELCOME TO FLORIDA." We are all amazed that we have made it this far and we are in our last state. It will take us 8 more days to pedal across Florida and arrive in St. Augustine. The beach traffic is starting to build, possibly because of spring break, and the weather is absolutely perfect.

Riding about two more miles, Zach stops and checks his rear tire to find he has a flat. Seems like 90% of the flats occur on the rear tire. We both jump on it and get it changed rather quickly. We pedal about five more miles before our SAG stop at Subway.

After lunch we reach the spot where 14 coasters gather for a side trip with John S. John calls ahead and arranges for permission to pedal onto Pensacola Naval Air Station to go to the museum on base. This is the home base for the Blue Angels Naval Air Pilots and we have to show our driver's license to get on base. We are about 7 miles off the Bubba route but will rejoin them later. The wind is with us all the way to the museum. The museum has an excellent display of military air history memorabilia from early flight years to the lunar landing. I climb into an F-14 simulator cockpit and have my picture taken. We are required to wear our tennis shoes and have to leave our bike shoes outside. I catch up with John the last hour and walk around with him for an education of his 20 plus years in the Air Force. He retired as a Lieutenant Colonel.

Upon leaving the museum, John looks at his rear tire and guess what? This is flat #16 for John, he is now leading the tour with the most flat tires. He has plenty of help in getting it changed. In just a short period of time, all 14 of us mount up and head to our sleeping destination at the new downtown Pensacola YMCA named for Bear Levin Studer. It's located at 165 East Intendencia Street. Located about twelve miles away, with the winds blowing at us in different directions, it should take us about an hour. The facility we are staying at was financed by Bubba Watson Pro Golfer Foundation Inc. We are allowed to bring our bicycles inside and put them in a back room. Our mattresses are waiting for us on the gym floor. Inside is nice; the north wall of the gym is all glass, floor to ceiling. Across the street there is a 6 story condo building.

Tomorrow morning is DSL day and believe it or not, I have my laundry list made out. This is becoming way too easy. Bubba has given Anne the night off again and he takes us all to dinner at a pizza restaurant. Most of us eat on the patio. Nancy and Peter from Columbus, join Zach and I at our table. We all learned quickly that when the sun goes down, so does the temperature. Tonight it's probably in the low 60s and windy.

Today has been a wonderful day. IT'S ALL GOOD. Something just crossed my mind, when I was young and attending St. Bernard's Grade School in Akron, Ohio from 1957 to 1965. I remember both my teachers Sister Joan OP and Sister Bernadine OP both saying I am doing well in class, except I need to work on my writing skills. Well here I am 60 years later writing about this trip of a lifetime. Thank you, Sisters, for the discipline and guidance.

Another random thought - The different parts of the country bring to mind different scents along the way. I think of the Bluebonnet flowers in East Texas and Louisiana as the logging trucks roared by us, and the familiar smell of southern yellow pine. The Bayou had a humid, almost musty smell. Now, coming into St. Augustine the smell of salt water brings back some memories.

Dauphin Island, Alabama

The Ohio Riders Cross Mobile Bay

JOURNAL DAY 45

Monday, April 15, 2019

Pensacola, Florida to Milton, Florida

31 miles

Last night we had our riders meeting in the hallway outside the YMCA gym. Bubba noted that the staff has requested that we be out of the building by 8:00 am so the members can use the facility.

Today is our 11th DSL day; I take a picture of the laundry I am sending.

Bubba also mentions stopping at the Waffle House where he will treat us to breakfast. I have another idea and I run it by Zach. I googled another restaurant, the Ruby Slipper, and it is close to Escambia Bay, located about a third of a mile from the YMCA. Zach agrees with me and we head out on our own. I have a southern breakfast. The tasty bread is made fresh on site.

Going back in my thoughts about 23 years, I remember being on board the USS FORRESTAL aircraft carrier for a Tiger cruise with my nephews, Steve and Tim and my brothers-in-law Dave and Helmut. The ship pulled into Pensacola Bay about two blocks from where we are eating breakfast. I would like to see the area and reminisce. That was the USS Forrestal's last cruise for sailors and civilians. It was decommissioned in 2015 and then dismantled in Brownsville, Texas.

With only 31 miles today, there is absolutely no rush to get to our campground for the night. We ride along Escambia Bay; the water is shimmering. It is another perfect day of riding and sun with no wind. The homes on both sides of FL- 90E are spectacular with their beautiful gardens and great views, any one of them could be in Better Homes and Gardens magazine.

Riding along a few of the coasters stop for a photo at a chimney. It is the remnants of the Jernigan Saw Mill that was constructed in 1830. It was a steam-powered sawmill that was destroyed during the Civil War. It was purchased and rebuilt and then closed again in 1920. If only this old chimney could talk....

Our lunch SAG stop at mile marker 24 is at the Shrimp Basket restaurant, where 14 of us arrive early and patiently wait for it to open. I have a Shrimp Po Boy Sandwich. Mmmm good.

After lunch we get back on US-90E and the traffic is heavy all the way to the KOA campground on Gulf Pine Drive. You can't miss the entrance to the campground with the huge black and yellow sign that reads, "WELCOME COASTERS." This KOA has many motorhomes that probably cost more than most normal homes in any area of the country. Many of these units also tow a vehicle and some of them even have a boat. I spoke with one couple from up north. They sold their home and bought a motorhome; they will travel the country until they get tired of it.

Today Jean and Bruce are able to rejoin us after Jean had a brief trip to the hospital.

Before dinner I have a discussion with Bob and Teri from Colorado about riding the C&O and Gap Trail from Pittsburgh to Washington D.C. They know I have ridden it twice. They are tandem riders and want to know if I can offer any information on that particular trail. I mention to them that the Gap is better riding than the C&O. In 2018 the C&O was rough even for a single rider.

After spotting my tent, I prop the bike up next to some bushes where I clean and oil my chain. Tonight we will pick up our 11th DSL. Thank goodness for Bubba and all the staff. Many thanks, you are all appreciated.

Reality is beginning to come to life for me. With only one week to go, we will finish this trip of a lifetime soon. Some days are hard, but we all know by day's end we will have a nice meal, hot shower, and a bed or 8" air mattress. So, guess what? "IT'S ALL GOOD!"

JOURNAL DAY 46

Tuesday, April 16, 2019

Milton, Florida to DeFuniak Springs, Florida

54 miles

The day has finally arrived when Mary is leaving Akron and driving south to meet me in St. Augustine, Florida. Mary's two sisters, Maggie and Cathy, will be traveling with her. They are taking time to stop overnight in Georgia to visit cousins and tour Savannah. While in Savannah, they plan to go to Leopold's Ice Cream; apparently it is the creamiest ice cream you will ever find.

Today we are routed on a lot of side roads that would make you think you are in Texas because of the rolling hills. We only have 54 miles ahead of today and normally that would be an easy day, but the elevation gain is 913 feet. The traffic is very light. While nothing exciting happens today, we know we are living the dream. By this time in the trip, we are pedaling, but don't think about it. It is like second nature; you and the bike are one.

Our first SAG stop is at mile marker 25 at a Tom Thumb gas station and store. I buy some orange flavored Gatorade. I drink half of it and mix the other half with my water so I can pitch the bottle. That gives me some zoom. We ride another hour and thirty minutes until mile marker 43, where we stop at the Simply Good Country Cooking Barbecue. It is just a little shack on the side of the road, but it is the best barbecue this side of the Mississippi, so far, in my opinion. It is not fancy, but simply good!

After lunch while riding through a residential neighborhood we have three visitors within a mile or so. Yes, you guessed it, all three have paws and all three like to chase something that goes around and around and that is the wheel on the bike. We all think they are just doing their jobs, barking and sometimes chasing us just to the boundaries of where they live. The one gray Pitbull chases us as if we have stolen his bone. The secret is to be prepared to switch gears and if you do it in time, you can outrun Fido. If you pass driveways with bushes lined alongside the drive, you need to stay on higher alert. It is like playing a game. It sure keeps us entertained and on our toes at a moment's notice.

Today's ride is not long, most coasters arrive around 1:00. Some of us early birds help the Wolf Pack set up the remaining tents. While riding into Sunset King RV Resort, I notice a nice inviting pool by the community center. After getting set up for the evening I decide to take a dip in the pool. I jump in a few times, swim a bit, then move over to the hot tub. That feels great on the old leg muscles. While walking back to camp, I notice several motorhomes that would be unbelievable places to rest your head. I think that is what they call "glamping." Glamour Camping, these people are definitely camping in style.

I stop at my bike to take my bag off for the night and I realize that my rear tire is flat. Tom, our SAG mechanic is set up in the same area and he motions for me to come over and put the bike on the rack. Within minutes he is finished and my bike is ready to ride tomorrow! Thanks Tom!

For this evening's meal, the women at the campground will be fixing us dinner and it will be held in their social hall. After dinner we have a local country entertainer come in and sing for us. A few of the cancer survivors from the group get up and sing a song. There are eight survivors among us. This is a very emotional, moving experience… to survive something like that and still pedal across the USA. I really haven't had any health issues at age 67, and surely nothing that compares to what these riders have had.

Journal Day 47

Wednesday, April 17, 2019

DeFuniak Springs, Florida to Marianna, Florida

68 miles

The residents at Sunset King RV Park, who are mostly snow birds, get up early to cook us a full breakfast this morning. We all thank them many times over. Temperatures last night were perfect for tent camping, it sure beats waking up and brushing frost off the tent, like we did five weeks ago.

At mile marker 9 on Circle Drive, we come upon the oldest library in Florida and it is the Walton DeFuniak Library, which opened in 1886. We stop to take a few pictures of the library and some Victorian homes that circle the lake. The homes are very well kept. They remind me of Thomas Kinkade paintings.

Today's weather is once again perfect, even if we have a little bit of a sidewind coming from the south. The roads we have been on for the last couple weeks are smooth, nothing like some of the roads in Arizona and Texas.

Several of us stop along a lake to take pictures and a Heinz 57 variety dog comes up from behind us and just sits and looks at us. After we start pedaling the dog starts following us. After a half hour and 8 miles later, the dog is still following us into our SAG stop. The dog never follows us out of the SAG stop. Pedaling on for about a mile a Chihuahua comes bolting off his front porch after us. I have to laugh, because I don't think he is going to cause much damage, being only 4 lbs., which is about what I ate for breakfast! Just kidding. The little dog does not have enough stamina to keep up with us, so we bid him farewell.

At mile marker 47 we have a SAG lunch stop at Bailey's Surf and Turf. They don't open until 11:00 and we wait very patiently for 20 minutes. I order a shrimp dinner. Can you imagine pedaling 47 miles and having to wait to eat? Exactly! LOL.

Today we are pedaling on FL-90 E for 57 miles and most of the time it is medium to high traffic volume. At times we pedal through a forested area. We can see the destruction of the forests that were decimated by Hurricane Michael in October of 2018. What it reminds me of is someone taking a huge sword and cutting the trees 25-30 feet above the ground. I talk with a logger about trying to retrieve the trees. He concludes, it would not be economically profitable. It would be like untangling spaghetti.

Riding along the highway 90 East, the traffic picks up and when we make it to the town of Marianna, Zach and I stop at a frozen yogurt business. Our purchase is weighed and it costs so much per ounce. Boy did that ice cold yogurt hit the spot once again.

Tonight's stay will be at Arrowhead Camp Resort where Hurricane Michael did extensive damage by taking out numerous trees and the Community Center. Since then a new Community Center has been erected and it is very nice. After a hot shower and dinner, we gather at the Pampered Zone where one of the riders, Timi Jo, announces she is a first time grandmother. Suddenly 4 bottles of champagne appear and we all congratulate her. She is disappointed she was not at the birth, but she used FaceTime as a tool to keep in touch with her family.

Hayes Baggett

Usually Bubba has a speaker come in once a week or so. Tonight's speaker is the Chief of Police of Marianna, Florida, Hayes Baggett. His talk is very informative in regards to Hurricane Michael. Chief Baggett said the good thing was they knew they were going to get a direct hit so they had a little time to prepare before. After the hurricane hit he said most streets were impassable due to debris and glass and any low lying areas were flooded. Slowly but surely, they are getting their lives back together.

Just an interesting fact, any time the Wolf Pack sets up the tents, they are always on the lookout for any fire ant hills (some as big as a basketball). If they find any they are instructed to put bleach on it. No one ever had an incident with the ants that I am aware of.

We have great reception with the internet because we are close to Interstate 10, so I FaceTime Mary, then Nick, Kristin and the grandchildren, Camden and Emory.

THE TIME OF MY LIFE

JOURNAL DAY 48

Thursday, April 18, 2019

Marianna, Florida to Tallahassee, Florida

85 miles

Today will be a longer riding day than most. At the meeting last night, Bubba suggested leaving earlier because of the heat and the distance. As I mentioned earlier in my journal, the SAG team puts biodegradable hot pink arrows on the road at a lot of the intersections for us to follow. The arrows are a great help especially in busy traffic.

About a mile before our first SAG stop, we see bright yellow arrows on the pavement pointing North. If you choose to, you can take this route into the state of Georgia and visit your ninth state. A few of us make the left turn on the road and down a steep hill and then up another hill and then we reach the Georgia state line sign. Zach and I take a few pictures and along come Bob and Teri our tandem riders. Getting back on our route we soon stop at our first SAG stop at the Around the Corner Eatery, at mile marker 25.

Today we have many left and right turns. This is Bubba's tenth year riding across the country and he has always picked the safest route possible whenever he could.

Our SAG check in at Courthouse Square is in Quincy, at Damfino's Cafe Market and Eatery, where we have lunch. I have a pulled pork sandwich. It is delicious. Once again at the restaurant things move pretty slowly, but to us it doesn't matter because it is air conditioned. It is early afternoon and we finally reach our last time zone, Eastern Standard Time.

At mile marker 63, we enter Orchard Pond Parkway, a brand new toll road that goes on for about 5 miles, but bikes are free. It is a road in the middle of nowhere and none of us can understand why it was built. There are no homes or structures. Just after we make our exit, the road just ends.

Our next SAG check in is mile marker 70, a Shell Gas Station. We are told to be very cautious because this is a high traffic area. Today I am drinking a lot of liquids, about 5 quarts. I took two Ibuprofen in the morning because of the length of the day and the +2,631 feet of climb.

Riding along on new Rt 90 E. we pass the bridge that was remnants of the old Rt 90. I stop to take a picture, and in one sense it looks like a piece of artwork of the days gone by.

After dinner tonight in the parking lot, Bubba gives each of us a surprise. We all receive a black t-shirt with white lettering on it, saying it is the worst weather trip in 10 years of his coast to coast travels. It reads, We Survived the strong winds, heavy rains, steep hills, snow, heat, sleet, hail and freezing temperatures on C2C, 2019. Thanks Bubba. There is a discussion about tomorrow's weather and what time we will leave, because of a strong, slow moving weather front coming off the Gulf of Mexico.

Tonight's stay at the Quality Inn is greatly appreciated because of storms in the area.

This evening I post on Instagram, FaceTime the grandkids, call Bob in Akron, Peter in Lakewood, Colorado, and Jack and Judy in Illinois.

A little input on our 52 nights, Bubba provides microfiber towels and washcloths on all nights except for hotel nights. When we finish with these towels we can use them to wipe off our bikes, or shoes or discard them.

THE TIME OF MY LIFE
JOURNAL DAY 49

Friday, April 19, 2019

Tallahassee, Florida to Live Oak, Florida

77 miles

The rain storm of which Bubba spoke last evening is currently over us as we eat breakfast at the Quality Inn. Bubba is in a staff meeting just off the hotel lobby. The result of this meeting determines that we can ride today with a little delay. We start riding out close to 9:30. Today's route will be primarily on US 90 E, a main road that should be open with no flooding. Today is just one of those days where you sit in the saddle and pedal and forget about the weather, today is just a wet riding day.

Remember, this is Florida and our elevation gain is 1,635 ft. Yes, even though Florida is considered flat we are still rolling. Between mile markers 22 and 35 the roads flatten out for a while and we are pedaling on flat pavement.

We stop in Greenville, where most of us pay tribute to Ray Charles, a famous American musician. At Haffye Hayes Park, in the center of town, there is a statue of Ray not far from his boyhood home. His most popular song was, "Georgia on my Mind." He started losing his vision as a child at 6 years old due to glaucoma. Ray attended the Florida School for the Deaf and Blind in St. Augustine from 1937-1945. Ray Charles had a very successful music career. He died from liver cancer on June 10, 2004.

We pass over the Swanee River. If you put on your thinking caps you may remember who wrote the song, "Old Folks at Home" also known as "Swanee River." Stephen Foster wrote the song in 1851, and it became the state song of Florida in 1935.

This day is not exciting in any way because of the weather. It's just rain, rain and more rain. The thunder and lightning passed over us just before our start this morning and we are now left with the rain. Today is one of the days that you want to forget, SAG stops, turns, lunch, you just spend the entire day looking forward to a nice hot shower, dry clothes and of course dinner. Tonight we are sleeping at the Suwannee County Fairgrounds in a gym setting in Live Oak, Florida.

On most evenings we can purchase beer or wine for a nominal fee, Bubba assures us he is not making money it is just an extra service. No purchases are made when we are at the schools, churches, or National Guard Armories.

JOURNAL DAY 50

Saturday, April 20, 2019

Live Oak, Florida to Gainesville, Florida

81 miles

I can't believe this trip of a lifetime is coming to a close. It's hard to believe this is the day before Easter Sunday. Our general direction today is southeast, once again we will have numerous left and right turns. We will have 1,261 feet of elevation gain on our way to Gainesville. Everyone thinks of Florida as being a flat state, but it is not.

Zach left early this morning to meet his wife, who is driving down from New Jersey for an overnight visit. She will go to Palatka then on to St. Augustine to see him finish the ride. This is Zach's second C2C trip with Bubba.

Our first SAG stop is at the Busy Bee Gas station at mile marker 16.9. I purchase a small Gatorade and an energy bar. Traffic today is very light on the backroads. The weather is very favorable today, sunny and warm. Our second SAG stop is at mile 39, at the Store/Canoe rental. Behind the store is a campground but it is for tents only.

O'Leno State Park

Riding on another eight miles, we make a left turn and pick up the Ichetucknee Trail. The storm last night left many branches on the trail, so we reroute to a road that runs parallel to the trail. The trail cuts through O'Leno State Park. I stop a few times and take pictures. The photo I take is of a dead tree O'Leno State Park with a unique shape and it is a resting place for many birds. Another photo is a fire tower in the park, which has the bluest blue sky as a background. Life is Good!

Lunch is at the Great Outdoors Restaurant in the town of High Springs. Teri and Bob from Colorado invite me to eat lunch with them. I have a four-cheese grilled sandwich, with 2 glasses of water. (In my mind, I hear Mary's voice say "Don't just drink coffee.")

Over the last few days the logging trucks have diminished which is a good thing and eases some of the stress.

Let's talk briefly about Bubba's strict safety rules. We are required to have front and rear lights. The rear red light is to be flashing at all times. He supplies all riders with a fluorescent lime green reflective safety vest, which is to be worn anytime we are on the bicycle. Another safety feature required at all times is a bike helmet. Bubba also requests that we give loud audible signals of left and right turns and loudly announce any road hazards we see and point to it.

Tonight's stay will be at the North Central Florida YMCA in Gainesville, on NW 34th Blvd.

After dinner, dessert and our meeting, Bubba's dog Buddy, finally, after 51 days comes up to me with the ball in his mouth and wants to play fetch. So, I throw the ball with Buddy for about 30 minutes. I am sure Buddy will sleep real well tonight, I know I will.

THE TIME OF MY LIFE

JOURNAL DAY 51

Sunday, April 22, 2019

Gainesville, Florida to Palatka, Florida

53 miles

EASTER SUNDAY

The Easter bunny is very sneaky, he came to visit when everyone was sleeping. We all wake up and find a bunny with an egg filled with candies. This brings back childhood memories of what our Easter mornings were like when I was a young. We would have to find our Easter baskets hidden in the house, then my dad would drive us in his 1957 Ford, to Easter Sunday Mass at St. Bernard's Church in Akron. Being on this tour with Bubba is only the second time I have been away from home on Easter. The first time happened when I was in the Army in 1971 and stationed at Ft. Knox, Kentucky, in cook school. The military occupational specialty for a cook is MOS 92G.

Since today is Sunday and especially Easter Sunday, the Devotional Service today will be the last one on our bike trip. We all gather on a couple picnic tables and Beth read passages from the Bible about Christ's Resurrection. There are a few new faces in the crowd this morning and Beth always has a gifted way with words.

Today's ride is a short one at 53 miles, we estimate only 3-4 hours actual ride time in the saddle. John S. wants to ride one day with me on the tour and we chose this day. John is one of those riders that usually prefers to ride alone. He rides a little faster than me but probably because of his age and he has longer legs than me. And, he's just a youngster at 63. A couple days ago John approached me about riding together the entire day, especially since Zach took off early to meet his wife, and I gladly accepted his offer.

After leaving the YMCA, we ride a short distance and see a Starbucks, with a lot of bicycles and of course we know who owns these. So we both shake our heads up and down and pull in with the rest of the group and have coffee and chat with the locals. A few of the locals ask, "Where are you going and where have you been?" We tell them where we started, and mention that we only have 90 more miles to go. They say they can't imagine pedaling across America. We explain to them we took the entire trip one day at a time and after the second week it just became a way of life. Well, until now, now we are in our last week and will be done tomorrow.

Early on Bubba encouraged us to talk to the locals, ask them what they did for a living and what there was to see in the area, after that, the conversations flow. Talking with an older gentleman 65-70 years old in Mississippi we had learned that he just installed a bathroom in his home for the first time, which meant he finally closed down his outhouse for good. Remember, this is 2019!

How fortunate we are in this great land of ours; we have all of these conveniences and we don't think a thing of it. Think about the song, GOD BLESS AMERICA, and all the times we sing it, next time dwell on the words. Freedom is not free, especially if you have any military ties. It's a good practice when you see or meet a Veteran, look at them and say, "Thank you for your service."

Today is a "take your time" day, because we cannot get into the National Guard Armory in Palatka until 2:00 pm. John and I are the very last to leave Starbucks. After a half hour of road riding 7.6 miles, we turn onto the Guerry- Hawthorne Connection Trail. We stay on the trail for 17 miles. This trail is very similar to the Erie Canal Trail close to my home in Ohio, except for a few things, and two of them come to mind right away. This trail has palm trees and alligators. Thirty minutes into our ride we come across Lochloosa Wildlife Conservation Area. John and I decide to check out the exhibits and walk on the wooden boardwalk that meanders through the swamp groves. It is a very nice sunny Easter Sunday and there are quite a few walkers on the trail. I think for a moment – we have traveled close to 3,000 miles and never locked our bikes. I make a comment to John about locking our bikes and we decide it is a good idea. Tomorrow is our last day and you just never know what will happen, better safe than sorry. So I put a cable lock on both bikes and attach it to the bike rack.

Walking on the trail we encounter a sign, "OPEN RANGE Bison, Horses, Alligators Free Roaming, DO NOT FEED OR APPROACH." During our walk we talk with a couple Naturalists who are very informed about this conservation area. One of my questions is, "Where are the alligators, we have not seen any"? And her response is, "They have seen you!"

We mount up once again and ride to the end of the trail where we stop for a restroom break. As I walk back toward my bike, I hear my phone ringing in my bag, I answer and it is Tom from the SAG support team. He has two questions for me, the first one is, "Where are you?" And the second question, "Is John S. with you?" I tell him we are two minutes away and yes John S. is with me. Arriving at our only SAG stop on this short day, PaPow makes me my go-to wrap, which is sliced banana, dill pickle, peanut butter and Smuckers jelly from Orville, Ohio. Of course, I wash this all down with a shot of dill pickle juice.

Riding along another fourteen miles, we see a group of coasters at Subway, so we stop in for a snack of a cookie and a chocolate milk.

Once again, the locals ask, "Where are you going?" Once again, we tell them and again we get that same look! Another question we hear is, "You have been pedaling for two months or seven and a half weeks?" and our answer is always, "yes!"

Leaving Subway, John S. and I approach FL-20E which is the main highway to Palatka. We pedal along at up to 18 mph at times. We pass a few coasters and one of Bubba's vehicles, which is stopped on the side of the road and we think nothing of it. Later in the day we learn Mike B. took a spill on his bike, which ended his ride into the beach tomorrow, our last day.

Arriving at the Palatka, Florida National Guard Armory, I take a shower, dress for the evening, make up my bed and head outside. I spot Anne setting up the snacks for the afternoon so I meander over to find a tasty morsel or two. The food is good and it's no wonder that even though I pedaled all this way, I have not lost any weight.

I call my old Army buddy Gary H., from Alliance, Ohio and tell him we are staying in a National Guard Armory. Gary and I spent 6 years in the Army Reserve as cooks. After my phone call with Gary, I stop to talk to the Recruiting Sergeant to see if I can re-up. (Age 68) We both have a good laugh. The Recruiting Sergeant asks me about our travels across the country and I give him a few of the high points. He says he is interested in taking a trip like this someday.

Anne will have our EASTER dinner ready for us at 6:00 pm. On the menu is a traditional Easter meal of Ham, Chicken, mashed potatoes, green beans, salad, quinoa and dessert. This is the last dinner Anne will prepare for us. Great Job, Anne and Serge, you are really appreciated.

After dessert, Bubba gathers the riders in a large circle and shares his thoughts on the trip. He mentions the weather we endured; it was unbelievable! He comments on how well we came together as a group, compared to being strangers at the start. This reminds me of the first riders meeting, it's hard to believe it's our last one. Bubba, along with his faithful dog Buddy, stood in front of us and gave us an emotional talk. At that time he told us this happens two days on the trip, the first day and the last day. There are 55 people gathered tonight and 42 are riders. We all applaud Bubba for what he did to get us safely across the United States of America. After Bubba finishes, it is our turn as riders to individually stand up and say what this trip has meant to us personally. Bubba announces we will start with our first rider and that just happens to be me. Getting off my chair and walking toward Bubba at the center of the circle, we embrace and I have to scramble my thoughts on what I want to say. It is hard to control my emotions. I first thank the staff and Bubba for the trip of a lifetime and for all the fantastic pampering. Then I thank my fellow riders for always being there. They were so helpful and encouraging - from fixing a flat to helping you keep a positive outlook. I recall a few days that would have been tough for any rider due to the strong headwinds and rain blowing directly in your face, but their complaints were few and far between. After I finish speaking, Bubba hands me a plaque with a picture of all of us on the first day, when we left Dog Beach in San Diego, California. We also receive a nice riding jersey that each of us will wear tomorrow for our final day of the trip and our arrival at the Atlantic Ocean and the beach at St. Augustine, Florida. This last meeting lasts more than two hours. As each rider is announced, there are hoots and hollers and much support for each other until the last rider is finished. Bubba gets up again and says each one of us has earned the right to wear this jersey. He officially welcomes us to the Coast 2 Coast family.

Earlier in the day Mike B. took a spill and they sent him to hospital to get checked out. Mike says this is his second C2C with Bubba and he is disappointed that he doesn't get to finish. He returns in time for the riders meeting and is moving very slow. After the meeting I ask Mike if he needs anything. He says he would like some help getting set up for the night. I help him get set up, and grab a vinyl chair for him to help him in the shower.

Tonight, lights out will be a half hour later at 9:30. I am posting pictures on Instagram and happen to look around our 70 x 90 gymnasium bedroom. I notice most riders are wearing the riders jersey Bubba just gave us; it appears they are going to wear them all night. When we parade to the beach tomorrow Gregg will lead the pack of riders. We chose him because he showed so much courage in taking on this trip with limited eyesight and he maintained a great positive attitude. Congratulations to you Gregg!

Before I fall asleep I reflect once again on this time. I am so happy that I decided to make this journey across America - I never want to say "Gee, I wish I would have done that." And every single night of our 52-night trip, we had a hot shower. In addition to that, every 4-5 days we had our DSL dirty stinking laundry done for us… 12 times! In the words of Bubba, "IT'S ALL GOOD!"

THE TIME OF MY LIFE

JOURNAL DAY 52

Monday, April 22, 2019

Palatka, Florida to St. Augustine, Florida

36 miles

Last night, going to bed felt like Christmas Eve night when I was a kid, as I tried to fall asleep I could hear others were not sleeping either. After 52 days we are getting anxious to get to the beach and relax. Most of us slept with our riding jerseys on, it is something special like when we were kids. Wearing the jersey, it is quicker getting dressed this morning. Today will be our last riding day. This will be our last breakfast together, as the group that started 7-1/2 weeks ago.

Now, it seems like the last seven weeks went by very fast. A few of us help the WOLF PACK this morning by folding up air mattresses. We only have 36 miles to go, we have plenty of time and we will get to St. Augustine in approximately 3 hours. It's a beautiful sunny morning with temperatures around 70 degrees and a cloudless sky.

As we leave the National Guard Armory, the pace is on the slower side, we all have the look on our faces that in a few short hours our ride across America will come to an end. Zach stayed with his wife Diane again last night and meets up with us just before we cross over the St. Johns River Bridge. At about mile marker 7, Zach remembers he has his wife's car keys in his pocket! Zach tells me to just go ahead, he will catch up with me later. He calls his wife Diane, and calls one of the SAG team members, and the three of them coordinate getting the keys back to his wife. Kudos to the support staff once again!

We are pedaling on a paved trail from mile marker 2 thru 20. At the end of this trail is our first and only SAG stop of the day, and our last SAG of the trip. We only have 16 more road miles to go, on the Palatka /Saint Augustine Trail to get to the ocean at St. Augustine

Beach. At mile marker 31 there is the sign, WELCOME TO ST. AUGUSTINE founded in 1565, America's oldest city. After seeing that sign my legs just stop pedaling and can't believe we are almost finished. That same lump I had in my throat on the first day comes back, 52 days later. My thoughts are on the past 52 days on what we all have done together; the experience feels like a dream.

The time is 10:30 am and we arrive in St. Augustine. Pedaling down King Street, the traffic is heavy. All of a sudden, I hear people hooting and hollering and I know we have reached our lunch gathering destination at A1A Ale- works. I park my bike on the railing next to the alley, and we walk upstairs to join the other bikers on the second floor balcony, where hugs and high fives are given. Joining the other riders on the balcony to watch the parade of riders as they pedal into town, even the locals and the tourists walking through town are cheering on the bikers. After almost all the riders are in, we order lunch.

Just as I finish ordering my lunch, Bubba announces more riders are coming. I stand to join the others who are already at the railing. As I look over, I hear someone yell, "Hey Bechter!" I look down at the traffic and spot Mary's Subaru with my nephew Tim looking up and waving through the open sun roof. Mary is driving, and in the back seat are her sisters Mag and Cathy along with Tim's wife Teresa. I yell out loud, "Hey that's my nephew and my wife is driving that car!" John S. glances over to me, "What's going on over there, that's the loudest you have been on the entire trip!" This is a great surprise!! I had no idea Tim and Teresa are here to see me in to the beach.

We leave A1A Ale Works at 12:30. John, Zach and I are the first riders to go over the Bridge of Lions on our way to McDonalds. We all meet and form a line to ride into the beach together. We are not required to wear the lime green fluorescent safety vest for our last 2 miles. We leave our bikes and walk across the road to the median strip where there's a large WELCOME TO ST. AUGUSTINE sign. We all gather in front with the flags of the countries represented for a final group picture. I am in the lower right corner of the banner.

Final Group Photo – St. Augustine, Florida

April 22, 2019

After pictures, Bubba groups us together and lines us up behind the support vehicle. As you may remember, Gregg has been selected to be the lead rider to take us to the beach. Because of his limited sight, he is truly an inspiration to all of us. Congrats to you, Gregg.

Only two more miles to go. Turning into a residential neighborhood, people are on the curb by the road cheering us on, they all know why we are here and what we have just accomplished. By this time, we can all smell the ocean air. As I make a right turn onto Route A1A, I can see the Atlantic Ocean come into view. I am sure all of us are on cloud nine. I look ahead and spot the Marriott Hotel where we will be staying. As we get closer to making the final left turn down to the beach, there are a couple dozen people standing by the road cheering us on. All of a sudden, I hear my name shouted to the right and I look over and see my niece Teresa, then my name is shouted out on my left, there is my nephew Tim, he yells out, "nice tan Bechter." I smile and try to hold back my emotions because the trip of a lifetime is almost over and Mary is waiting for me.

Making the final left turn on 7th street, we reach our destination and I have to get off of my Jamis bike for the last time and walk it single file with the other riders over the wooden boardwalk, to get to the beach. Half way over the boardwalk I spot my wife Mary with a camera and a phone in her hand taking pictures. I stop quickly for a hug and a kiss. Boy am I glad to see her, this was the longest we have been separated since we met 34 yrs. ago. I keep the line moving over the walkway, and the next two people I know are my sisters-in-law, Mag and Cathy standing on the beach. And there it is, 100 feet in front of me, the Atlantic Ocean. Words cannot describe the emotions, when I see relatives take time out of their busy lives to be here, to give support for me in achieving this once in a lifetime goal. I will never forget this moment.

Shoes and socks come off, and into the ocean I go with my bike for the dipping of the front wheel which now makes it OFFICIAL! Mission Accomplished. I completed 52 days riding my bike from Coast 2 Coast. I pick up my Jamis bike and hold it over my head for a celebration picture.

After about 15 minutes of visiting, the riders have one more thing to do at the beach with Bubba. All bikers line up and walk up to Bubba one at a time. He throws his arms around you, shares some words of wisdom and support, for you only, and thanks you for doing the ride. One of his SAG members hands him a red, white and blue striped lanyard from which hangs a 3 inch gold medal and Bubba places it around my neck. The inscription on the medal reads 2019 Coast to Coast 10th Anniversary.

Lots of people are already gathered on the beach, family and friends, and it is difficult to say goodbye to the other coasters in the confusion. I feel like Forrest Gump. After all this pedaling I finally stop at the ocean, and just turn around. The Marriott where we are staying is just across the street on A1A Highway. We start to filter over to the hotel. I take a shower and a short nap before we get ready for dinner. Mary is in the room with me reading on the bed. When I wake up she asks me if I am done pedaling my bicycle because I was pedaling in my sleep. She tells me the bed started shaking and it scared her, until she realized my legs were moving in my sleep like I was still on the bicycle.

While getting ready to go to dinner it occurs to me I won't have to ride my bike tomorrow or the next day. This became a routine after 7- 1/2 weeks. When we started this trip, it took me a week to get into the rhythm of things, after that I was living a dream. At night before falling asleep, I thank God for this incredible adventure.

Our celebration dinner is on Highway A1A at the Sunset Grill. Most riders with family and or friends are there. We have St. Louis ribs, full rack, falling off the bone tender with the perfect barbecue sauce, and a loaded baked potato. The other option is a white fish and both are excellent choices. At the restaurant for the first time Bubba is on the quiet side. "What a great guy you are Bubba, everything that you told us is true." Remember the old western, *Wagon Train* with Ward Bond? Well Bubba reminds me of him as our wagon master.

After dinner we walk back to the Marriott for a pool party and celebration with glasses of champagne and a gathering around the fire pit. I meet Bubba's sister Grace who works at the office in Tampa, Florida. Well, this adventure has to end sometime and as I look back, I will always think, WOW I did the trip that has been in my dreams for decades.

Anne, our culinary chef, is at the party with Serge, and gives all the riders a copy of her cookbook, which has some of the dishes she prepared during our trip. I ask for two copies, one for my sister-in-law Maggie and a signed copy for us. I try to move around and say goodbye to fellow riders. While saying goodbye to Otto from Germany, Tim my nephew, walks over and I introduce him to Otto. Tim is a Subway owner and he asks Otto if there are Subways near his home in Germany and he replied, "Ya." Then Tim asks, "What could Subway do to be better?" Otto responded, "There are too many selections to choose from." After a few minutes of listening to Otto it becomes comical. He talks about the choices of breads, then meats, then vegetables, it is almost a standup comedy act and we all laugh. A bit later, John S. comes over to our table and we all talk awhile. About 10:30 we all agree it is time to retire. Today was a short riding day but long otherwise, mostly emotional. IT'S ALL GOOD!

THE TIME OF MY LIFE
POST RIDE REFLECTION
APRIL 23 - MAY 1, 2019

Waking up Tuesday morning at the Marriott, before jumping out of bed, Mary and I talked about the ride being over, after 52 days. Mary stated last night as I was sleeping my legs were going like I was pedaling. After a shower we met Mary's sisters Mag and Cathy, her niece Teresa and nephew Tim for breakfast across the street at Obis Restaurant. After breakfast I went back to the hotel to make a few connections with coasters before they left the hotel. I gave Sherri and Zach a bottle of my homemade wine that Mary transported from home.

The family decides to tour Old Town St. Augustine to see the sights and different shops. Upon Tim's recommendation we all had lunch at the famous Columbia Spanish restaurant, founded in 1905 by a Cuban Immigrant, Casimiro Hernandez, Sr. It's Florida's oldest and the largest Spanish Restaurant in the world and the menu is extensive. We all had their famous Sangria and raised our glasses to celebrate a coast to coast pedaling adventure from ocean to ocean.

After enjoying a leisurely lunch together, we went back to hotel. Mary's family finished packing and the four of them headed to the airport. I was at a loss for words in thanking them all for coming to see me ride into the beach, very appreciative.

After they left, Mary and I went to the St. Augustine Beach lighthouse, toured the museum and climbed 219 steps to the top for a fantastic view. From the top you could see the 36 miles to Palatka where the coast to coasters spent our last night. For dinner Mary and I went to O.C. Whites Seafood which was also recommended by Tim. It was a nice evening, good food, nice atmosphere, great weather. We ate in the courtyard and listened to a local entertainer.

Wednesday, I was probably the last coaster at the Marriott Hotel. Mary and I left early and went to Mass at the Cathedral Basilica of St.

Augustine in old town. Then we went to breakfast a couple doors down to the east, at the Athena Restaurant. St. Augustine is the oldest city in the United States, it was founded in 1565 by Pedro Menendez and has a lot of history and old world charm.

After breakfast we toured the old town shops. We walked to Flagler College to take the tour of the famous buildings and campus which comprises 19 acres which was previously known as the Ponce De Leon Hotel. Another recommendation by Tim. Henry Flagler the Railroad Magnate had this hotel constructed. We saw the original, ornate, Tiffany stained glass windows in the Dining hall and some of the period furniture pieces. Late in the afternoon we took a drive down the historic A1A Highway south to the Cinnamon beach area with the windows down to take in the scenery and ocean air before heading back to St. Augustine for dinner. The one place we wanted to try again was the Columbia Spanish Restaurant, we really enjoyed the food. After having a Sangria, we decided to purchase a one of a kind, handmade Sangria pitcher for Tim and Teresa.

Thursday, we packed up and went to breakfast at the Maple Street Cafe across from Flagler College. Then we headed north to Savannah Georgia, some 180 miles. We arrived in time for lunch at Huey's New Orleans Cafe on 115 East River Street Savannah. With a view of the river, we watched as many large vessels came and went loaded with railroad shipping containers stacked 6 high. We took our own self walking tour of the town and stopped for an ice cream at the famous Leopold's Ice Cream Parlor, circa 1919. We toured The Cathedral of St. John the Baptist, and walked through Chippewa Square Park where the movie, Forest Gump was partially filmed.

Friday, after breakfast we headed north to Charleston, South Carolina, another 107 miles. We stayed at The Meeting Street Inn, established in 1874, just four blocks from the Charleston Harbor. After checking in, we toured the Slave Market and had lunch at Hyman's Seafood which is owned by 4th and 5th generation family members. The seafood, hush puppies and boiled peanuts were prepared southern style and it is a very popular place to go. After lunch we went for a carriage ride with the Carolina Polo Carriage Company.

Saturday morning, we had breakfast in the courtyard at the Inn by the water fountain. It was so relaxing. We had tickets to go to the Magnolia Plantation which was established on the Ashley River in 1676 by Thomas and Ann Drayton. We toured the house, beautiful gardens and grounds. It was a peaceful setting except for the calls of the numerous Peacocks that were walking around the grounds. They had a petting zoo where we spent time walking with the animals. I made friends with a large goose that insisted on staying next to me and sitting on my foot to be petted and talked to. The large peacocks were everywhere. We eventually headed north on Highway 17 to Myrtle Beach South Carolina, 102 miles, where we had reserved a room at the Hampton Inn.

Sunday, we called Aunt Betty and made plans to have breakfast with her, her daughter Debbie and husband George. I shared my recent coast to coast ride with them and we reminisced about the many years gone by. When we left Aunt Betty, we stopped at Our Lady by the Sea Catholic Church to visit the grave of Uncle Emidio. The next couple days were spent just relaxing on the beach. We had a great dinner at the Sea Captain's House and went to a fantastic show at the Carolina Opry on RT 17 in Myrtle Beach. These past few days were very relaxing in body, mind and soul.

But if the truth be known, it was time to go home. I was ready after over two months on the road that covered 13 states.

In life, a lot of things can be taken from you, but the experience of pedaling a bicycle coast to coast will stay with me forever and words cannot ever describe it. One will never fully know what a trip means or does to a person until a ride like that is finished. It was truly the time of my life and an experience I will never regret.

CLARENCE BECHTER

Clarence Bechter B515490@Aol.com

In my younger years, a seed was planted with a thought to ride my bicycle across the USA from sea to shining sea. As the years passed, some of life and responsibilities became more important, my family and my life's work. At the ripe young age of 62, I started mountain climbing and within a few years I had reached the summit of eleven ,14,000 foot peaks, including Mount Whitney in California. At the age of 67 years, I discovered Bubba's Pampered Peddlers and made the decision to go with his tour group in the winter of 2019. My wife Mary gave me her blessing, to live out my dream of some 55 years, she reminded me that I have spent my whole life doing for others. Now it's time for me to do what I always dreamed of. I dedicated each day to people in my family and in my life who have influenced and supported me in my ride across the country. The list grew to over 100, and I had 52 days to fit everyone in.

Day 1 was dedicated to the Father, Son, and Holy Spirit.

Day 2 was for my understanding partner in life, my wife Mary.

Day 3 was for my son, Nick, and his wife, Kristin, and our grandchildren, Camden and Emory.

Bubbas tour was everything I dreamed of and truly was an adventure of a lifetime. I hope you enjoyed reading this as much as I enjoyed riding coast to coast.

www.ingramcontent.com/pod-product-compliance
Lightning Source LLC
Chambersburg PA
CBHW041453010526
44107CB00013B/1031